Options for Strengthening All-Source Intelligence

Substantive Change Is Within Reach

CORTNEY WEINBAUM, BRADLEY KNOPP, SOO KIM, YULIYA SHOKH

Prepared for the Office of the Secretary of Defense
Approved for public release; distribution unlimited

RAND | NATIONAL DEFENSE RESEARCH INSTITUTE

For more information on this publication, visit **www.rand.org/t/RRA1245-1**.

About RAND

The RAND Corporation is a research organization that develops solutions to public policy challenges to help make communities throughout the world safer and more secure, healthier and more prosperous. RAND is nonprofit, nonpartisan, and committed to the public interest. To learn more about RAND, visit www.rand.org.

Research Integrity

Our mission to help improve policy and decisionmaking through research and analysis is enabled through our core values of quality and objectivity and our unwavering commitment to the highest level of integrity and ethical behavior. To help ensure our research and analysis are rigorous, objective, and nonpartisan, we subject our research publications to a robust and exacting quality-assurance process; avoid both the appearance and reality of financial and other conflicts of interest through staff training, project screening, and a policy of mandatory disclosure; and pursue transparency in our research engagements through our commitment to the open publication of our research findings and recommendations, disclosure of the source of funding of published research, and policies to ensure intellectual independence. For more information, visit www.rand.org/about/principles.

RAND's publications do not necessarily reflect the opinions of its research clients and sponsors.

Library of Congress Cataloging-in-Publication Data is available for this publication.
ISBN: 978-1-9774-0885-3

Cover: freshidea/AdobeStock.

About This Report

Foreign attacks against the United States occur frequently, but the American people, U.S. policymakers, and even some intelligence analysts have become inured to the rising temperature of these national security threats. The current environment demands prompt consideration of changes to intelligence structures and authorities that would enable intelligence analysts to become aware of foreign interference and disinformation campaigns sooner; ensure the dissemination of unclassified intelligence assessments to everyone who needs access to them, including private sector organizations; and protect against politicization.

This exploratory study sought to address these needs by proposing Big Ideas—game-changing ideas that, while bold and audacious, are also implementable without requiring major intelligence reform. We reviewed previous intelligence reforms and scholarly literature to understand earlier proposals, and we conducted 17 interviews with current and former U.S. and foreign intelligence leaders, practitioners, and scholars to ask what they would change if they could, which barriers need to be lifted, and where the greatest opportunities for meaningful change in the intelligence community reside.

The research reported here was completed in August 2021 and underwent security review with the sponsor and the Defense Office of Prepublication and Security Review before public release.

RAND National Security Research Division

This research was sponsored by the Office of the Secretary of Defense and conducted within the International Security and Defense Policy Center of the RAND National Security Research Division (NSRD), which operates the RAND National Defense Research Institute (NDRI), a federally funded research and development center (FFRDC) sponsored by the Office of the Secretary of Defense, the Joint Staff, the Unified Combatant Commands, the Navy, the Marine Corps, the defense agencies, and the defense intelligence enterprise.

For more information on the RAND International Security and Defense Policy Center, see www.rand.org/nsrd/isdp or contact the director (contact information is provided on the webpage).

Acknowledgments

We thank Richard Girven and Anthony Vassalo for their support of this project. We are grateful to all of the intelligence leaders and practitioners who participated in this study and who generously shared their time and perspectives with us. Thank you to our reviewers Molly Dunigan, Richard Girven, and Alan Pino for their comments, which without doubt sharpened our thinking and improved the quality of this report.

Summary

Foreign attacks against the United States occur frequently, but the American people, U.S. policymakers, and even some intelligence analysts have become inured to the rising temperature of these national security threats. The intelligence community (IC) has been slow to notice Chinese and Russian disinformation campaigns surrounding the coronavirus disease 2019 (COVID-19) and its vaccines, and the IC takes a reactive stance regarding persistent, large-scale attacks against U.S. cyber infrastructures and intellectual property. Meanwhile, the IC has neglected domestic threats, too, such as its failure to issue a threat assessment warning of potential violence targeting the Capitol on January 6, 2021.[1] U.S. intelligence exists to provide intelligence collection and analysis to advise leaders and protect U.S. national security interests, yet many signs indicate that the IC is failing at this role while ignoring the intelligence needs of national security stakeholders in the private sector.

Drawing from our research, we assert that the current environment demands prompt examination and consideration of changes to intelligence structures and authorities that would enable intelligence analysts to become aware of foreign interference and disinformation campaigns sooner; ensure the dissemination of unclassified intelligence assessments to everyone who needs access to them, including private sector organizations, members of Congress who do not serve on national security oversight committees, and the American public; and protect against politicization.

This exploratory study sought to propose Big Ideas—game-changing ideas that, while bold and audacious, are also implementable without requiring major intelligence reform. We conducted 17 interviews with current and former U.S. and foreign intelligence leaders, practitioners, and scholars to ask what they would change if they could, which barriers need to be lifted, and where the greatest opportunities for meaningful change in the IC reside. We reviewed previous intelligence reforms to understand earlier proposals, and, drawing from that review and the results from government commissions and panels, scholarly articles, and other literature, we identified ideas that could meet today's challenges.

Through our extensive literature review, which included the evaluation of several congressional and presidential commissions empaneled to review intelligence operations and structures, and our interviews with a select group of U.S. and allied intelligence experts, we found broad agreement that

- the IC does not adequately use open-source intelligence (OSINT)
- guardrails against politicization offer insufficient protection against the influence of political bias on intelligence analysis and dissemination
- nongovernmental sectors—the commercial sector, academic and scientific sector, and the American public—are increasingly the "attack surface" on which foreign adversaries wage their attacks, and these nongovernmental sectors are making decisions that affect national security without the benefit of intelligence threat assessments
- U.S. structures and organizations for protecting the homeland by warning against such attacks are inadequate.

Our goal for this report is to stimulate debate that leads to changes that strengthen U.S. national security against adversaries who are exploiting U.S. enterprises.

---

[1] Committee on Homeland Security and Governmental Affairs and the Committee on Rules and Administration, *Examining the U.S. Capitol Attack: A Review of the Security, Planning, and Response Failures on January 6*, staff report, Washington, D.C.: U.S. Senate, June 8, 2021, p. 1.

Opportunities for Meaningful Change in the Intelligence Community

This report presents two Big Ideas that offer radical change for intelligence, and each is supported by our report's findings.

Big Idea 1: Create a New Organization Responsible for Unclassified Data (Collection) and Open-Source Intelligence (Analysis)

An overwhelming conclusion from our research is that intelligence analysis still relies too heavily on classified information, even in areas where unclassified data are more prevalent and would provide a fuller understanding of an issue. Furthermore, comprehensive unclassified reporting built on a foundation of tradecraft standards would offer a remedy (though not a panacea) against politicization by providing a baseline of intelligence to all policymakers, regardless of the user's security clearance level. Open-source information (or publicly available information [PAI]) and tradecraft remain stovepiped in the Open Source Enterprise (OSE), deprioritized by OSE's parent organization (the Central Intelligence Agency [CIA]), unevenly available across organizations and offices, or inaccessible, and the role of an OSINT functional manager is absent.[2]

A solution to overcome these challenges could be the creation of an organization that is *dedicated to the collection and analysis of open sources*. We recommend that this new organization serve as an OSINT functional manager through two distinct directorates to resolve challenges associated with the collection and analysis of open-source data.

Directorate One would manage data-purchase agreements and PAI collection on behalf of the IC to provide agencies with access to data in accordance with such agreements.[3] This directorate would identify and prioritize data sets that are of greatest intelligence value. This directorate would have a civil liberties staff that is responsible for determining which data can be used and stored by the IC and which data can be shared with which agencies under which terms (e.g., if data are de-identified). This directorate would also be responsible for developing and implementing tradecraft to assess the credibility of data sources.

Directorate Two would conduct analysis on the data collected by Directorate One. This OSINT analysis would employ different tradecraft and skills than those used by Directorate One.[4] Directorate Two would employ data scientists, financial analysts, geopolitical analysts, linguists, data visualization experts, and other experts to create OSINT products that can be used by members of other agencies, such as all-source analysts in the IC, law enforcement officers in federal and state agencies, and other users. Some of this directorate's products would have controlled dissemination (controlled unclassified information) and others would be publicly released. Publicly released products may or may not include sourcing information.

The entire mission of OSE should be subsumed into this new organization, which would significantly and substantively expand OSE's current functions and activities. In fact, the creation of this new organization may render OSE no longer necessary, allowing those positions and resources to be redirected.

Some who have argued over the years for an increased role for OSINT in the IC have also argued that so-called *exquisite capabilities*—those collection capabilities that are unique to the IC and not commer-

---

[2] In this study, we use *OSINT* to refer to intelligence derived from open-source information; we use the terms *open-source information* or *PAI* to refer to information that has not yet been analyzed.

[3] This would exclude publicly or commercially available geospatial intelligence (GEOINT) or signals intelligence (SIGINT), which would remain with their respective functional managers.

[4] This analytic role would be comparable to the National Security Agency's role in conducting SIGINT analysis or the National Geospatial-Intelligence Agency's role in conducting imagery analysis.

cially available—should be saved for those essential topics on which OSINT cannot report.[5] However, until the IC truly invests in OSINT across the range of intelligence topic areas, the community will not know for sure which topics can be covered adequately with OSINT to allow such exquisite collection to focus on the remaining hard targets. Meanwhile, others have argued that the IC should be restricted in its collection of publicly available and commercially available data sets. Centralizing this function in one agency would allow for more-focused congressional oversight than the current landscape provides when every agency has its own approach.

Big Idea 2: Provide Intelligence as a Service to the American Public

The IC conducts activities that are necessary "for the conduct of foreign relations and the protection of the national security of the United States."[6] When the foreign threat is already inside U.S. borders, the IC's mission should be even more important. Threats to the U.S. homeland include threats to the American public, the U.S. commercial sector, and the U.S. scientific and research ecosystem—all of which require national security protection. The Director of National Intelligence (DNI) could modify Intelligence Community Directive (ICD) 191, which asserts a "duty to warn" both U.S. and non-U.S. persons of threats of violence against them, particularly threats of death and kidnapping.[7] The DNI could expand ICD 191 to include nonviolent threats as well, such as cyberattacks, intellectual property theft, and manipulation through disinformation campaigns. Our research found no statutory limitation that requires the DNI to restrict the duty-to-warn directive to threats of physical violence.

This change would create the policy environment required to provide intelligence to the public, but it would not realign missions or structures. The DNI would have several options next. Without creating a new organization, current all-source analytic organizations could write products for public dissemination, and early candidate topics could include analysis on cyber threat trends, disinformation trends, and foreign talent programs. After the first few such products are released, ODNI could establish mechanisms for scaling this capability based on early lessons learned. Or, a second option is that the DNI could establish or assign an organization to disseminate unclassified intelligence products and threat assessments to public audiences. This organization would be separate from that described in Big Idea 1, because it would rely on all-source intelligence rather than a single-source discipline. It could operate similarly to the Congressional Research Service in that it would publish public reports based on both its own initiative and in response to specific tasks assigned by its management.

Implementation of Big Idea 2 should not be significantly hindered by funding concerns. The requirement to provide intelligence services to the public is already embedded in laws and regulations, especially those authorizing elements of the Department of Homeland Security (DHS), and the existing analytic review process can be used for all-source analytic products identified for public release during the initial years.

---

[5] James M. Davitch, "Open Sources for the Information Age: Or How I Learned to Stop Worrying and Love Unclassified Data," *Joint Force Quarterly*, Vol. 87, 4th Quarter 2017; Sandra Jontz, "The Intelligence Everyone Can See," *SIGNAL*, September 1, 2017.

[6] Executive Order 12333, *United States Intelligence Activities*, December 4, 1981, as amended by Executive Orders 13284 (2003), 13355 (2004) and 13470 (2008).

[7] Intelligence Community Directive 191, *Duty to Warn*, Washington, D.C.: Office of the Director of National Intelligence, July 21, 2015.

Conclusion

Our study was not originally designed to focus on OSINT, but as we asked one person after another how to overcome politicization (sunlight is the best disinfectant), how to monitor foreign adversary activities in the United States (use open sources), and how to reveal these activities to affected Americans and commercial entities (publicly release intelligence), all roads led to OSINT. Other changes are needed, too, but what we learned is that *substantive* change for the IC does not require major overhaul and reform, and even these Big Ideas are well within reach.

Contents

CHAPTER ONE

The Water Is Boiling

Over the past 80 years, many U.S. intelligence reforms have been made in response to intelligence failures, partisan politics and distrust of intelligence, or a combination of the two.[1] The intelligence failures that led to the September 11, 2001, terrorist attacks on the United States and the failure to find weapons of mass destruction in Iraq both provided impetus for major reforms—the Patriot Act of 2001 and the Intelligence Reform and Terrorism Prevention Act of 2004, respectively—while leaks of sensitive information by Chelsea Manning in 2010 and Edward Snowden in 2013 led to more-modest reforms, including amendments to the Foreign Intelligence Surveillance Act of 1978. Intelligence reforms often occur in response to a public outcry, and they sometimes include innovative ideas that may not be implemented for years or even decades.[2]

Although changes have occurred in the structure and organization of intelligence agencies, the intelligence community (IC) continues to face long-standing challenges related to collaboration, the use of open sources, analytic tradecraft, and the risk of politicization. It might be tempting to believe that these challenges are persistent and enduring and that, short of a cataclysmic intelligence failure, significant reforms are not needed. However, such a viewpoint would ignore the fact that *the water is already boiling*: Foreign attacks against the United States occur frequently, but there has been no corresponding urgency from the public or elected officials to demand intelligence that warns of such threats or informs response options.

For example, in 2014, Russia interfered with elections in Ukraine,[3] developing a playbook that they would use in 2016 during the UK's European Union membership referendum (Brexit);[4] Russia used it again in 2017 during the lead-up to the French presidential election.[5] Yet within this period, in 2016, Russia interfered in the U.S. presidential election by proliferating disinformation online[6] and by hacking the Democratic National Committee.[7] In response, U.S. elected officials described not being adequately warned of Russia's

---

[1] Glenn Hastedt, "The Schlesinger Report: Its Place in Past, Present and Future Studies of Improving Intelligence Analysis," *Intelligence and National Security,* Vol. 24, No. 3, 2009, p. 423.

[2] The Schlesinger Report recommended the creation of a Director of National Intelligence (DNI) decades before the position was actually created (Brent Durbin, *The CIA and the Politics of US Intelligence Reform*, Cambridge, United Kingdom: Cambridge University Press, 2017, pp. 106–119).

[3] Ukrainian Election Task Force, *Foreign Interference in Ukraine's Democracy*, Washington, D.C.: Atlantic Council, May 2019.

[4] Rachel Ellehuus and Donatienne Ruy, "Did Russia Influence Brexit?," *Center for Strategic and International Studies*, July 21, 2020.

[5] Jean-Baptiste Jeangène Vilmer and Heather A. Conley, *Successfully Countering Russian Electoral Interference: 15 Lessons Learned from the Macron Leaks*, CSIS Brief, Washington, D.C.: Center for Strategic and International Studies, June 2018.

[6] William Marcellino, Christian Johnson, Marek N. Posard, and Todd C. Helmus, *Foreign Interference in the 2020 Election: Tools for Detecting Online Election Interference*, Santa Monica, Calif.: RAND Corporation, RR-A704-2, 2020.

[7] Office of the Director of National Intelligence (ODNI), "Background to 'Assessing Russian Activities and Intentions in Recent US Elections': The Analytic Process and Cyber Incident Attribution," in ODNI, 2017; Marek N. Posard, Marta Kepe, Hilary Reininger, James V. Marrone, Todd C. Helmus, and Jordan R. Reimer, *From Consensus to Conflict: Understanding Foreign Measures Targeting U.S. Elections*, Santa Monica, Calif.: RAND Corporation, RR-A704-1, 2020.

interference in U.S. elections by the IC.[8] In the years since then, Russia and China have both peddled false information about the coronavirus disease 2019 (COVID-19) and vaccine safety, accusing the United States of developing and intentionally spreading the virus,[9] and they have claimed that the vaccines are not safe.[10] Yet these false narratives were not fully understood until after many Americans had decided that they would not get vaccinated at any cost.[11] As of April 2021, 13 percent of U.S. adults reported that they will "definitely not" get the COVID-19 vaccine, and this rate was the same for both Black and White Americans, indicating that these results cannot simply be attributed to distrust of medical research and practices among communities of color. Eighty-four percent of adults who have said that they will "definitely not" get the COVID-19 vaccine believe that the vaccines "are not as safe as they are said to be," which indicates their agreement with views proliferated through disinformation.[12] Although Russia and China are not the sole purveyors of such disinformation, they are engaging in a modern form of biological warfare against the United States by using disinformation and propaganda to encourage the spread of this deadly virus. We believe that the IC's role in warning the American public against these attacks has been inadequate.

Other attacks are targeting the U.S. commercial and research-and-development sectors. Under current intelligence policy, the IC is not responsible for providing intelligence to private-sector organizations, which leaves these organizations vulnerable to foreign economic attacks. The Federal Bureau of Investigation (FBI) and the National Counterintelligence and Security Center estimate that China steals U.S. intellectual property, trade secrets, and innovations, and it counterfeits goods worth approximately $400 billion per year.[13] The magnitude of these attacks on U.S. economic security can hardly be overstated, yet the commercial sector and the scientific research sector (industry, academia, and nongovernmental organizations) do not receive intelligence threat assessments that might help them protect their organizations. In the absence of such data, leaders in these sectors are unable to make informed decisions on how to protect their organizations, their operations, and their data.

Other threats are internal to the IC, where the risk of politicization is growing. Intelligence leaders whom we interviewed reported that, during the Trump administration, analysts chose to omit the word "climate" from intelligence and chose which intelligence to publish based on their perceptions of how the President or his advisors might perceive their intelligence reports. Although concerns about politicization might not be new—the cherry-picking of intelligence was identified as a cause of the Iraq war[14]—shaping intelligence

---

[8] Susan B. Glasser, "Ex-Spy Chief: Russia's Election Hacking Was an 'Intelligence Failure,'" *Global Politico*, podcast transcript, December 11, 2017; Select Committee on Intelligence, *Report of the Select Committee on Intelligence, United States Senate, on Russian Active Measures Campaigns and Interference in the 2016 U.S. Election*, Vol. 1: *Russian Efforts Against Election Infrastructure with Additional Views*, 116th Congress, redacted report, Washington, D.C., date redacted.

[9] Miriam Matthews, Katya Migacheva, and Ryan Andrew Brown, *Superspreaders of Malign and Subversive Information on COVID-19: Russian and Chinese Efforts Targeting the United States*, Santa Monica, Calif.: RAND Corporation, RR-A112-11, 2021.

[10] Global Engagement Center, *GEC Special Report: Pillars of Russia's Disinformation and Propaganda Ecosystem*, Washington, D.C.: U.S. Department of State, August 2020.

[11] Matthews, Migacheva, and Brown, 2021.

[12] Liz Hamel, Lunna Lopes, Grace Sparks, Mellisha Stokes, and Mollyann Brodie, "KFF COVID-19 Vaccine Monitor: April 2021," polling findings, Kaiser Family Foundation, May 6, 2021.

[13] FBI, *Executive Summary—China: The Risk to Corporate America*, Washington, D.C., undated; William Evanina, "Threat Briefing," in *China Initiative Conference*, video, Center for Strategic and International Studies, February 6, 2020, 10:00 minutes.

[14] Walter Pincus, "Ex-CIA Official Faults Use of Data on Iraq; Intelligence 'Misused' to Justify War, He Says," *Washington Post*, February 10, 2006.

reports according to what might be expected to play well politically cannot reasonably be considered appropriate tradecraft in any era.

Focus of This Study

The current environment demands prompt examination and consideration of changes to intelligence structures and authorities that would enable intelligence analysts to become aware of foreign interference and disinformation campaigns sooner; ensure the dissemination of unclassified intelligence assessments to everyone who needs access to them, including private sector organizations, members of Congress who do not serve on national security oversight committees, and the American public; and protect against the types of politicization that has occurred in recent years.

This exploratory study was designed to address these needs by proposing ideas and solutions that, while bold and audacious, are also implementable and achievable. These Big Ideas that we propose are potential game changers: They offer *meaningful, significant,* and *substantive* changes that are *politically feasible* without requiring major reform. In government, *achievable* often means *incremental,* but incremental improvements will not adequately address current problems in the IC. The IC has spent several decades trying to figure out how to adequately gather and use publicly available information (PAI) and has spent even more time training intelligence officers to resist politicization. Previous studies, interviews conducted during this study, and a "deep dive" conducted in 2020 by the House Permanent Select Committee on Intelligence (HPSCI) all have demonstrated that incremental changes and self-management have not resulted in sufficient improvements.[15]

Instead of proposing incremental change, we focus on changes that represent a clear shift in current practice in key areas and that can be implemented all at once. However, we are not proposing an overhaul of U.S. intelligence along the lines of the major intelligence reforms that emerged in our literature review. We are proposing actionable Big Ideas whose implementation *are well within reach.*

Approach

Our team first reviewed historical attempts at intelligence reform to understand which ideas were implemented, which ideas had value but their time had not yet come, and which drivers for reform existed in prior eras compared with the drivers that exist today. We then conducted a series of unstructured interviews with 17 current and former U.S. and foreign intelligence leaders, practitioners, and scholars. We chose our interview subjects based on their access to the challenges that we examined: people who have been in the room when decisions are made that determine the boundary between foreign and domestic intelligence collection; officials who have had active roles in creating the analytic tradecraft in use today—across the civilian and defense analytic cadres—and who have mentored a generation of intelligence analysts in the use of such tradecraft; officials who have participated in discussions about which intelligence to present or not present to the President and how those decisions were made; officials who have experience with congressional intelligence committees—including recent experiences about which they may speak more openly than current officials would feel comfortable doing; and, finally, foreign officials who can discuss how their own countries address any or all of these issues. Our choice of which governments to include in our study was based solely

---

[15] HPSCI, *The China Deep Dive: A Report on the Intelligence Community's Capabilities and Competencies with Respect to the People's Republic of China,* unclassified executive summary, Washington, D.C., September 2020.

on selecting democratic governments whose values closely align to U.S. values and civil liberties, as well as foreign governments whose officials might be well informed about the IC, such that they can make relevant comparisons and references.

Table 1 lists the names and positions of those interview participants who gave us permission to publish their names; we interviewed one additional person who asked not to be named in this report. All interviews were conducted under the agreement that we would not attribute any comments, findings, or ideas presented in this document to any persons on this list. We are grateful to these participants for sharing their experiences with us.

Finally, we searched for other ideas and strategic thinking that thought leaders in intelligence have published in recent years. Many books, journal articles, research reports, and other prestigious publications have tackled similar questions to those addressed in our study. We list those sources from which we extracted value in the references section at the end of this report. In many cases, the ideas drawn from these publica-

TABLE 1
Interview Participants (in Alphabetical Order)

Name	Relevant Position
Joseph Gartin	former Chief Learning Officer, Central Intelligence Agency (CIA)
Sue Gordon	former Principal Deputy Director of National Intelligence
Larry Hanauer	Vice President for Policy at the Intelligence and National Security Alliance; former senior staff member of HPSCI
Emily Harding	Deputy Director of the International Security Program at the Center for Strategic and International Studies; former deputy staff director at the Senate Select Committee on Intelligence (SSCI)
Mike Hughes	First Assistant Director General and senior intelligence officer in the Australia Office of National Intelligence; briefer to the prime minister and foreign minister
Catherine Johnston	Vice Director of Intelligence for Indo-Pacific Command (INDOPACOM); former Director of Analysis, Defense Intelligence Agency (DIA)
Jason Klitenic	national security practice leader at Holland & Knight; former General Counsel, ODNI
Katrina Mulligan	Principal Deputy Assistant Secretary of Defense for Special Operations and Low Intensity Conflict; former attorney adviser and director for preparedness and response in the National Security Division at the U.S. Department of Justice; former director for disclosures response at the National Security Council
Kathy Pherson	CEO of Pherson Associates, LLC; coauthor of the book *Critical Thinking for Strategic Intelligence*
Randy Pherson	President of Pherson Associates, LLC; coauthor of three books on intelligence analysis
Shelby Pierson	Intelligence Community Election Threats Executive; principal adviser to the DNI on threats to elections and election security
Paul Rimmer	former Deputy Chief of UK Defense Intelligence
Beth Sanner	former President's daily briefer; former counselor to the National Intelligence Council
Anthony Vassalo	IC liaison for the RAND Corporation; former Associate Deputy Director of National Intelligence for Mission Integration
Neil Wiley	former Chair of the National Intelligence Council; former Director of Analysis, DIA
William Wu	Deputy Staff Director, SSCI

NOTE: One additional person asked not to be identified.

tions provided fertile soil in which our team's ideas grew during this project. Therefore, taken together, they framed our thinking and shaped this report.

Organization of This Report

The remainder of this report takes a "bottom line up front" approach. We present our Big Ideas first, then describe the findings that led to them. The findings are organized into five topic categories. We conclude by describing how these findings informed the Big Ideas presented in this report and provide a set of additional ideas that warrant future research and further discussion, although they are not yet ready for implementation.

CHAPTER TWO

Big Ideas Within Reach

Our goal was to identify Big Ideas that are bold enough to make meaningful change and realistic enough to be implemented within the current political landscape. The two ideas described below were shaped by the findings from our interviews and other research, as described in the following chapter. These ideas build on the *spirit* of previous intelligence reforms using what we learned during this study.

Big Idea 1: Create a New Organization Responsible for Unclassified Data (Collection) and Open-Source Intelligence (Analysis)

An overwhelming conclusion from our research is that intelligence analysis still relies too heavily on classified information, even in areas where unclassified data are more prevalent and would provide a fuller understanding of an issue. Furthermore, comprehensive unclassified reporting built on a foundation of tradecraft standards would offer a remedy (though not a panacea) against politicization by providing a baseline of intelligence to all policymakers, regardless of the user's security clearance level. Open-source information (or PAI) and tradecraft remain stovepiped in the Open Source Enterprise (OSE), deprioritized by OSE's parent organization (CIA), unevenly available across organizations and offices, or inaccessible, and the role of an open-source intelligence (OSINT) functional manager is absent.[1]

A solution to overcome these challenges could be the creation of an organization that is *dedicated to the collection and analysis of open sources.* We recommend that this new organization serve as an OSINT functional manager through two distinct directorates to resolve challenges associated with the collection and analysis of open-source data, which we describe in the following chapter.

Directorate One would manage data-purchase agreements and PAI collection on behalf of the IC to provide agencies with access to data in accordance with such agreements.[2] This directorate would identify and prioritize data sets that are of greatest intelligence value. This directorate would have a civil liberties staff that is responsible for determining which data can be used and stored by the IC and which data can be shared with which agencies under which terms (e.g., if data are de-identified). This directorate would also be responsible for developing and implementing tradecraft to assess the credibility of data sources.

Directorate Two would conduct analysis on the data collected by Directorate One. This OSINT analysis would employ different tradecraft and skills than those used by Directorate One.[3] Directorate Two would employ data scientists, financial analysts, geopolitical analysts, linguists, data visualization experts, and other

---

[1] In this study, we use *OSINT* to refer to intelligence derived from open-source information; we use the terms *open-source information* or *PAI* to refer to information that has not yet been analyzed.

[2] This would exclude publicly or commercially available geospatial intelligence (GEOINT) or signals intelligence (SIGINT), which would remain with their respective functional managers.

[3] This analytic role would be comparable to the National Security Agency's role in conducting SIGINT analysis or the National Geospatial-Intelligence Agency's role in conducting imagery analysis.

experts to create OSINT products that can be used by members of other agencies, such as all-source analysts in the IC, law enforcement officers in federal and state agencies, and other users. Some of this directorate's products would have controlled dissemination (controlled unclassified information) and others would be publicly released. Publicly released products may or may not include sourcing information.

The entire mission of OSE should be subsumed into this new organization, which would significantly and substantively expand OSE's current functions and activities. In fact, the creation of this new organization may render OSE no longer necessary, allowing those positions and resources to be redirected.

Some who have argued over the years for an increased role for OSINT in the IC have also argued that so-called *exquisite capabilities*—those collection capabilities that are unique to the IC and not commercially available—should be saved for those essential topics on which OSINT cannot report.[4] However, until the IC truly invests in OSINT across the range of intelligence topic areas, the community will not know for sure which topics can be covered adequately with OSINT to allow such exquisite collection to focus on the remaining hard targets. Meanwhile, others have argued that the IC should be restricted in its collection of publicly available and commercially available data sets. Centralizing this function in one agency would allow for more-focused congressional oversight than the current landscape provides when every agency has its own approach.

Big Idea 2: Provide Intelligence as a Service to the American Public

The IC conducts activities that are necessary "for the conduct of foreign relations and the protection of the national security of the United States."[5] When the foreign threat is already inside U.S. borders, the IC's mission should be even more important. Threats to the U.S. homeland include threats to the American public, the U.S. commercial sector, and the U.S. scientific and research ecosystem—all of which require national security protection. The DNI could modify Intelligence Community Directive (ICD) 191, which asserts a "duty to warn" both U.S. and non-U.S. persons of threats of violence against them, particularly threats of death and kidnapping.[6] The DNI could expand ICD 191 to include nonviolent threats as well, such as cyber-attacks, intellectual property theft, and manipulation through disinformation campaigns. Our research found no statutory limitation that requires the DNI to restrict the duty-to-warn directive to threats of physical violence.

This change would create the policy environment required to provide intelligence to the public, but it would not realign missions or structures. The DNI would have several options next. Without creating a new organization, current all-source analytic organizations could write products for public dissemination, and early candidate topics could include analysis on cyber threat trends, disinformation trends, and foreign talent programs. After the first few such products are released, ODNI could establish mechanisms for scaling this capability based on early lessons learned. Or, a second option is that the DNI could establish or assign an organization to disseminate unclassified intelligence products and threat assessments to public audiences. This organization would be separate from that described in Big Idea 1, because it would rely on all-source intelligence rather than a single-source discipline. It could operate similarly to the Congressional Research

---

[4] James M. Davitch, "Open Sources for the Information Age: Or How I Learned to Stop Worrying and Love Unclassified Data," *Joint Force Quarterly*, Vol. 87, 4th Quarter, October 2017; Sandra Jontz, "The Intelligence Everyone Can See," *SIGNAL*, September 1, 2017.

[5] Executive Order 12333, *United States Intelligence Activities*, December 4, 1981, as amended by Executive Orders 13284 (2003), 13355 (2004), and 13470 (2008).

[6] Intelligence Community Directive 191, *Duty to Warn*, Washington, D.C.: Office of the Director of National Intelligence, July 21, 2015.

Service in that it would publish public reports based on both its own initiative and in response to specific tasks assigned by its management.

Implementation of Big Idea 2 should not be significantly hindered by funding concerns. The requirement to provide intelligence services to the public is already embedded in laws and regulations, especially those authorizing elements of the Department of Homeland Security (DHS), and the existing analytic review process can be used for all-source analytic products identified for public release during the initial years.

The remainder of this report discusses the research findings that led to these two potentially game-changing ideas, and the discussion of those findings includes additional ideas that may be worthy of further consideration and study.

CHAPTER THREE

Findings

Our research findings, presented in this chapter, came predominantly from interviews and our review of other documents, as noted. We drew upon these research findings to inform our Big Ideas, and we present our findings as they relate to five topics:

- framing the foundational challenges
- challenges in collecting and using open-source information
- nongovernmental entities are engaging in national security
- limitations of existing IC statutes and structures
- the politicization of intelligence.

Our findings indicate that the intelligence reforms of the past two decades led to significant changes in the IC, but these reforms were not enacted in ways that fully achieved the intentions and spirit of certain reforms. As a result, new *reforms*—such as major legislative action—may be unnecessary, while significant *changes* are still required. Our findings indicate that OSINT should be made available to all-source analysts, and this need is not being met today. Our findings also indicate a need for publicly released all-source analysis to inform a wider audience than that which currently receives IC assessments. Finally, our interviews and literature review suggest that decisions about which intelligence to deliver to which users have sometimes been informed by the perceived political bias of the recipients and that methods to mitigate this risk of bias could include providing unclassified intelligence to audiences who do not currently receive classified intelligence and providing opportunities, such as training, for senior IC leaders to encounter these challenges in facilitated environments.

Framing the Foundational Challenges

In 2020, HPSCI examined whether the IC was prepared for the range of threats posed by China, and it noted significant gaps in the IC's capabilities:

> The Committee's central finding of this report is that the United States' intelligence community has not sufficiently adapted to a changing geopolitical and technological environment increasingly shaped by a rising China and the growing importance of interlocking non-military transnational threats, such as global health, economic security, and climate change. **Absent a significant realignment of resources, the U.S. government and intelligence community will fail to achieve the outcomes required to enable continued U.S. competition with China on the global stage for decades to come, and to protect the U.S. health and security.** [emphasis in original][1]

---

[1] HPSCI, 2020, p. 8.

In particular, HPSCI noted gaps in the types of intelligence collected as well as an insufficient ability to integrate data from various sources. In its report, HPSCI questioned analysts' ability "to synthesize and assess disparate streams of information,"[2] and it described "insufficient emphasis and focus on 'soft,' often interconnected, long-term national security threats, such as infectious diseases of pandemic potential and climate change, and such threats' macroeconomic impacts on U.S. national security."[3] These concerns align with findings from our own interviews.

The Definition of "Intelligence" Is Evolving Although the IC Continues to Maintain a Narrow View of Its Scope

Intelligence leaders and scholars have debated whether the IC is at an "inflection point."[4] In discussions about recent national security events—such as Russian interference and covert influence in U.S. elections and attempts to trace the origin of the COVID-19 virus—one interview participant noted that the role of the IC is national security, not secrecy. In today's world, fulfilling this mission requires a broad view of what constitutes intelligence. For example, if Russia or China is disseminating anti-vaccine propaganda to the U.S. population, assessing the foreign sources of this information is within the mission of the IC—even if the data are solely available in unclassified open sources. The CIA webpage states the agency's mission simply: "Our mission is straightforward but critical: leverage the power of information to keep our Nation safe."[5] Nowhere on the CIA or DIA websites do we read that either agency should be restricted to assessing classified sources.

Yet the debate about what information constitutes *intelligence* is alive. One interview participant referred to the COVID-19 pandemic to illustrate this point, saying that the role of the IC is not to provide information or a viewpoint on the virus, but its role does include examining what the Chinese government knew about the virus and when they knew it.

Other interview participants focused less on the classification debate—how much the IC should rely on open sources—and instead accused intelligence agencies of having a bias for *actionable* intelligence. Some stated that intelligence analysts prefer to focus on topics that customers can act on—such as intelligence support to terrorism that might lead to operations or intelligence support to ongoing policy debates—rather than foundational intelligence, while others responded that "our customers don't want to hear what's not actionable." Whether this bias is driven by intelligence officers' desire to make an impact or desire to be closer to the action, according to interview participants, the IC pays insufficient attention both to topics that essentially require monitoring over long and uneventful periods of time and to topics for which no clear solutions exist (disinformation campaigns, for example).

Some of our interview participants acknowledged the challenge posed by an expanded definition of intelligence. One said, "Priorities, priorities, priorities. You can't do everything, and you can't do everything in detail." Although all interview participants might likely agree that intelligence agencies need to set priorities, they would probably have a harder time agreeing on which topics or functions should fall by the wayside. Existing prioritization mechanisms, including the National Intelligence Priorities Framework, have their advantages, but these create enduring challenges when a shift in priorities leads to decisions about whether to turn away from collection opportunities that will take ten years to rebuild.

---

[2] HPSCI, 2020, p. 8.

[3] HPSCI, 2020, p. 27.

[4] Joseph W. Gartin, "The Future of Analysis," *Studies in Intelligence,* Vol. 63, No. 2, June 2019, p. 1.

[5] CIA, "About CIA," webpage, undated.

All-Source Analysts Currently Do Not Have Access to All Necessary Sources of Information

Interviews revealed that OSINT continues to be deprioritized and underused across all-source intelligence. In most intelligence disciplines (INTs), a preference for one INT over another might be because of the nature of a particular intelligence topic (some topics are more readily monitored in one INT than in another). However, interview participants indicated that OSINT is underused even across topics that *should* be well suited to OSINT. Some speculated about possible root causes for the underuse of OSINT, including the lack of an OSINT functional manager and the long-standing debate about whether unclassified sources meet the threshold to be considered *intelligence*.

The notion that intelligence should not be limited to classified information is not new: In 1966, Sherman Kent observed that intelligence also includes "unromantic open-and-above-board observation and research."[6] In 1996, HPSCI reported that intelligence analysts *need and lack* sufficient access to unclassified sources.[7] Our interview participants echoed these concerns, noting that the IC lacks an enterprise-wide understanding of the publicly available data sources that exist and lacks tradecraft for how to assess, evaluate, and incorporate each type of data. These roles are currently dispersed across the IC—including CIA, DIA, the combatant commands, and elsewhere—with no one entity acting as the functional manager for OSINT by setting tradecraft standards or proliferating tradecraft expertise.

Although ICD 203 requires that all analytic products "shall be . . . based on all available sources of intelligence information,"[8] the reality described by interview participants is that analytic products are based on sources *collected* by the IC rather than the full range of sources that would have been *available* to the IC—should the IC have sought them out.

An interview participant said, "I don't know what all the answers are, [but] I know the outcomes we've got to have . . . we've got to use more info[rmation]." They continued, "What I don't want us to do is—because we can't figure out how to do it—we let ourselves off the hook." Philosophical debates ask how much unclassified data an *intelligence agency* should rely on before it has simply become a *research agency*, while practical debates ask why the IC has thus far been unable to capitalize on machine learning and other advanced technologies to process the volume and veracity of open-source data available.[9] An interview participant described the underuse of PAI in the following way:

> Do we adequately employ PAI? In short, the answer is no, but not because we don't value it. We don't employ it as effectively as it needs to be [employed] because, unlike SIGINT, GEOINT, and others, we don't treat the collection and production of OSINT as a separate discipline. As long as the IC OSINT effort is a modest OSE and a bunch of cottage industries scattered around the IC, we'll never bring OSINT into play in a way commensurate to its value in all-source assessment.

We discuss our OSINT-specific findings later in this chapter.

---

[6] Sherman Kent, *Strategic Intelligence for American World Policy*, Princeton, N.J.: Princeton University Press, 1966.

[7] HPSCI, *IC21: The Intelligence Community in the 21st Century*, staff study, Washington, D.C.: U.S. Government Printing Office, June 5, 1996.

[8] Intelligence Community Directive 203, *Analytic Standards*, Washington, D.C.: Office of the Director of National Intelligence, January 2, 2015; ODNI, "Objectivity," webpage, undated.

[9] Cortney Weinbaum and John N. T. Shanahan, "Intelligence in a Data-Driven Age," *Joint Force Quarterly*, Vol. 90, 3rd Quarter, July 2018.

Although Challenges Need to Be Addressed, There Is a Lack of Political Appetite for Major Intelligence Reform

Congress controls the IC's resourcing—in both dollars and number of positions—and neither Congress nor the executive branch has shown recent interest in major intelligence overhauls. Even if this assertion were not evident to us before this study began, it resonated clearly through our interviews and led to our focus on identifying changes to the IC that could be *meaningful, significant, substantive,* and *politically feasible* within Washington's current environment.

The reasons for this lack of appetite are numerous and not immediately linked to animosity between political parties or political ideologies. At the simplest level, barring a major crisis, the American public is not particularly interested in a major national security overhaul, and therefore, elected officials focus on other topics that voters care more about. Deeper reasons for this lack of appetite include an unwillingness by Congress to significantly raise the IC's budget and a lack of agreement on ideological issues, such as the role of the IC in domestic security or how the IC should collect and handle PAI.

A review of recent National Defense Authorization Acts indicates that officials are more willing to support narrowly focused changes, such as strengthening protections for civil liberties or adding funding to certain programs that counter China.

One interview participant suggested that reform might usefully start with a narrow topic that public officials on both sides of the aisle and the executive and legislative branches of government can support, such as better intelligence-sharing on cyber threats between the IC and the private sector. This participant further suggested that cyber might be one area in which new processes could be created (for producing and disseminating unclassified intelligence assessments, for example), and that successes in this area could be parlayed into other areas later. Another interview participant suggested that the biggest bang for the buck may come from reassessing how the IC assigns classification to analysis, including a review of security classification guides, or a reassessment of the underlying concepts of derivative classification that require every all-source product to be classified at the highest level of any one source, even when the assessment or judgment cannot be traced back to the specific source or method. Interview participants proposed these options as ideas that would create substantive improvements to intelligence production and dissemination without requiring major politically led reforms.

Challenges in Collecting and Using Open-Source Information

Previous attempts to increase the use of OSINT have not come to fruition. In 2005, the Commission on the Intelligence Capabilities of the United States Regarding Weapons of Mass Destruction (WMD Commission) made three recommendations regarding the use of OSINT. The first stated, "The DNI should create an Open Source Directorate in the CIA to use the Internet and modern information processing tools to greatly enhance the availability of open source information to analysts, collectors, and users of intelligence." The other two recommendations focused on creating an open-source analytic cadre and developing the ability to process large volumes of data.[10]

---

[10] Laurence H. Silberman, Charles S. Robb, Richard C. Levin, John McCain, Henry S. Rowen, Walter B. Slocombe, William O. Studeman, Patricia M. Wald, Charles M. Vest, and Lloyd Cutler, *The Commission on the Intelligence Capabilities of the United States Regarding Weapons of Mass Destruction: Report to the President of the United States*, unclassified version, Washington, D.C., March 31, 2005, pp. 568–569.
This same recommendation can be found in the 1996 HPSCI staff study (p. 568), which states,

> The IC must continue to develop improved means of collecting, exploiting and processing open-source information . . . and . . . [t]he IC must improve its ability to retrieve data from common databases. These databases must be checked thoroughly by

The recommendation to create an open-source directorate was enacted but not fully realized. That is, the DNI *did* create such a directorate within CIA, which is now called OSE, but OSE has not fulfilled the purpose envisioned for it, which we discuss further below. Several interview participants—and others who we did not interview,[11] including members of HPSCI[12]—may agree that the WMD Commission's recommendations remain relevant and unrealized.

For Many Topics, OSINT Provides Many Benefits, Including Speed, Relevance, and Utility

One benefit for the use of open sources is speed. According to interview participants, OSINT can often be shared quickly or can be shared with users who cannot access more highly classified intelligence.[13] This opportunity may lead to a potential pitfall, however: If an OSINT product is shared with a user who either does not have access to classified intelligence or who has simply not seen the related classified intelligence *yet*, the OSINT may mislead that user in the same way that a SIGINT or human intelligence (HUMINT) report taken out of context can be misleading.[14] One report from a single INT, without the benefit of all-source analysis, has the potential to lead a policymaker to a false conclusion. Some fear that the potential for such error is magnified with OSINT because a policymaker who reads a SIGINT or HUMINT report out of context presumably has the security clearance level to also read an all-source analytic product on the same topic, whereas this may not be true for an uncleared reader of OSINT.

One option to mitigate this risk is to take a handful of intelligence topics that are routinely discussed in classified all-source products and test how well OSINT analysts would cover the same topics. If the OSINT analysis is on par with the all-source analysis, perhaps these topics could be outsourced to OSINT, with occasional classified collection used to verify whether changes to the baseline analysis have occurred.

In addition to these benefits, OSINT provides an opportunity to share intelligence assessments with foreign partners, which allows that OSINT could be particularly useful in countering foreign disinformation. Department of Defense leaders, including the Deputy Assistant Secretary of Defense for Special Operations and Combating Terrorism, have emphasized the ongoing need for the United States to counter Russia, China, and other non-state actors that are "flooding the information environment with deliberately manipulated information that is mostly truthful with carefully crafted deceptive elements."[15] If the IC is unable to produce unclassified all-source products across the breadth of topics needed, OSINT provides an alternative. Either solution—unclassified all-source products or OSINT products—would be an improvement over the status

those responsible for requirements and analysis before new collection tasks are levied. Collection should be guided by the use of the least costly, most efficient and most productive means, whether overt or covert.

[11] See, for example, Zachery Tyson Brown and Carmen A. Medina, "The Declining Market for Secrets," *Foreign Affairs*, March 9, 2021; Amy Zegart, "The Moment of Reckoning: AI and the Future of US Intelligence," Hoover Institution, March 12, 2021a.; Brian Katz, "The Collection Edge: Harnessing Emerging Technologies for Intelligence Collection," CSIS Brief, Washington, D.C.: Center for Strategic and International Studies, July 2020.

[12] In September 2020, HPSCI released an unclassified executive summary that assesses the IC's ability to respond to China and recommends that "[a]n external entity should conduct a formal review of the governance of open-source intelligence (OSINT) within the intelligence community, and submit to congressional intelligence and appropriations committees a proposal to streamline and strengthen U.S. government capabilities" (HPSCI, 2020, p. 32).

[13] We remind readers that we use *OSINT* to refer to intelligence derived from open-source information; we use the terms *open source, open-source information*, or *PAI* to refer to information that has not yet been analyzed.

[14] Jason Vest and Robert Dreyfuss, "The Lie Factory," *Mother Jones*, January/February 2004.

[15] Chris Maier, then–acting Assistant Defense Secretary for Special Operations and Low Intensity Conflict, as quoted in Theresa Hitchens, "New Strategy Aims to Up DoD, IC Game to Counter Disinformation," *Breaking Defense*, March 16, 2021.

quo, according to the nine combatant commanders who wrote a letter to the DNI pleading for unclassified intelligence that they could share with partner nations.[16] However, we note that, even when unclassified intelligence might be useful to enhance foreign partnerships or might be able to counter Russian or Chinese influence, that information cannot be shared under current restrictions on disseminating intelligence. If the products were written for public distribution, these restrictions would become moot. We discuss this topic further in the section on broadening the definition of national security.

The IC Does Not Currently Possess All the Capabilities Needed to Analyze OSINT

Several interview participants noted that, unlike other INTs, including GEOINT, SIGINT, and HUMINT, OSINT is lacking in tradecraft. For example, in these other intelligence disciplines, collectors have a set of tradecraft that they can use to assess the credibility of sources, single-source analysts have a set of tradecraft that they use when reporting on collection, and this tradecraft can be shared with users who conduct their own collection at various military echelons or at other organizations. Interview participants with experience in overseeing all-source analysis reported that this is not occurring with OSINT and that the effects trickle down into analytic products. Previous RAND research explored existing uses of OSINT within the Department of Defense and detailed efforts made to develop methodology and tradecraft for it.[17] That study also indicated that OSINT lacks methodological rigor.

Interview participants reported a need for a similar tradecraft on both the collection and analysis of open sources. A task force at the Center for Strategic and International Studies identified specific tactics, techniques, and procedures (TTP) and technologies that could improve the collection, processing, and exploitation of OSINT.[18] Intelligence leaders whom we interviewed described a need for collection methods that assess the credibility of open sources, similar to how single-source analysts assess all other sources, and for analytic methods that are widely trained, repeatable, and rigorous. We note that interview participants did not overtly claim that OSE lacks such tradecraft; however, they perceived that, if such tradecraft exists, it has not been taught or proliferated outside OSE. The bottom line is that analysts at other agencies—including in combatant commands that are far from OSE both geographically and organizationally—do not have access to this knowledge for their daily use.

Interview participants noted that creating an open-source silo in a single organization—i.e., letting one agency be the OSINT silo that does all of this internally—would be a disservice to everyone involved. Some argued that it would be impossible to prevent intelligence officers outside that silo from conducting OSINT, but, without access to that organization's processes and skills, officers outside the silo would be conducting OSINT with poor tradecraft—essentially what is happening today. Another interview participant noted that creating such a silo would prevent analysts from seeking out OSINT because "they'd assume that someone else is doing it." As new forms of OSINT emerge—Internet-of-things devices and artificial intelligence–enabled technologies being two examples mentioned—analysts need a dedicated cadre of OSINT tradecraft experts who can create new methods for using new sources.

The roadmap for creating OSINT tradecraft exists, but too many interview participants expressed disappointment at the amount of progress that has occurred in the IC. They noted that multiple agencies—inside

---

[16] Hitchens, 2021; Betsy Woodruff Swan and Bryan Bender, "Spy Chiefs Look to Declassify Intel After Rare Plea from 4-Star Commanders," *Politico*, April 26, 2021.

[17] Heather J. Williams and Ilana Blum, *Defining Second Generation Open Source Intelligence (OSINT) for the Defense Enterprise*, Santa Monica, Calif.: RAND Corporation, RR-1964-OSD, 2018, p. 12.

[18] Katz, 2020.

and outside the IC—purchase the same data sources, creating redundant spending, without having the established tradecraft for assessing the credibility of these data sources.

Previous studies have examined OSINT and its uses. In a 2018 RAND study, Heather Williams and Ilana Blum examined the defense applications of OSINT and broke down "OSINT methodology and the operations cycle specific to each of its subtypes, laying out some common difficulties in each and efficiencies provided by new technological advancements."[19] Williams and Blum's study created a framework that defined first- and second-generation OSINT as follows: First-generation OSINT (the Foreign Broadcast Information Service [FBIS]) was built on translation expertise, often required physical access, had regular publication cycles, and focused on analysis and dissemination; second-generation OSINT (e.g., the Open Source Center) was built on technical expertise, virtual accessibility, constant acquisition, and a focus on exploitation and production.[20] Their report forecasted a third-generation OSINT, which would be "built on machine learning and automated reasoning [and] pervasive encryption denying access" with a "focus on collection and dissemination."[21] Their 2018 forecast for OSINT has been realized, but without either the policies or the tradecraft required to fully benefit from the emergence of this intelligence.

Finally, a much-discussed challenge with open-source information is how to handle civil liberties and privacy concerns when the government is collecting and purchasing public or commercial data sets. Today, lawyers at different agencies reportedly disagree over the IC's use of data sets—interview participants noted that a data set that is approved by lawyers at one agency can be rejected by lawyers at another agency because of different interpretations of the same laws. An organization that centralizes OSINT tradecraft could—and should—also centralize decisions about how specific data sets should be used and how to manage the protection of individuals' data. A so-called "clearing house for commercial info," as one interview participant described it, would prevent the government from unnecessarily "buying the same information over and over again, and the entity would have a privacy filter for each agency."

Open-Source Is Not Working, It Is Not Getting Better, and the Open Source Enterprise Had Ample Opportunity to Change

A key purpose behind the establishment of OSE was to "enhance the availability of open-source information to analysts, collectors, and users of intelligence."[22] However, OSE has often gone in the opposite direction, deprioritizing the need to provide OSINT to people outside the IC. For example, in June 2019, OSE decommissioned its unclassified website on the dot-gov domain. This decision cut off the many non-IC audiences who were regular users of the OSE website, including the U.S.-China Economic and Security Review Commission (USCC), which, in November of that year, recommended to Congress that ODNI "restore the unclassified Open Source Enterprise website to all of its original functions for U.S. government employees."[23] When the website was still not restored nearly two years later, David Logan, in his testimony before USCC,

---

[19] Williams and Blum, 2018, p. ix.

[20] Williams and Blum, 2018, p. 40.

[21] Williams and Blum, 2018, p. 40.

[22] Silberman et al., 2005, p. 377.

[23] U.S.-China Economic and Security Review Commission, "Comprehensive List of the Commission's Recommendations," in *2019 Report to Congress of the U.S.-China Economic and Security Review Commission*, Washington, D.C.: U.S. Government Publishing Office, November 2019.

Four members of Congress have co-sponsored a bill that would create an $80 million federally funded research and development center to translate foreign documents into English. If enacted, this bill would provide vital translation capabilities, filling just one necessary function for OSINT analysis (Joaquin Castro, "Congressman Castro Introduces Bipartisan Bill to Create China and Russian Translation and Analysis Center," press release, Washington, D.C., July 28, 2021).

explained the value of the information that OSE had previously provided to researchers studying China and the detriment of the organization's decision to decommission its public-facing website:

> Open-source research, including from military reporting, news media, PLA [People's Liberation Army] doctrinal and curricular materials, public-facing government documents, and academic reports, is incredibly valuable to better understanding China's nuclear weapons programs, including the roles China assigns to its theater nuclear weapons systems, the drivers and future trajectory of China's nuclear forces, and the role of the emerging air and sea legs of China's nuclear triad. However, the U.S. government has erected obstacles to open-source research. In June 2019, the Open Source Enterprise (OSE) was decommissioned and its contents transferred to restricted networks. The OSE had previously provided valuable access to open source information about the Chinese military and its nuclear forces. This access is particularly valuable given the increasing challenges of conducting fieldwork in China.[24]

The challenge with OSE is not its lack of a public-facing website; rather, its decision indicates how OSE has deprioritized providing OSINT to people who need it. One of our interview participants explained that the director of OSE "doesn't have the right authorities" to act as a functional manager for OSINT. In other words, if OSE is not required to provide information to anyone except CIA analysts, then OSE or CIA or ODNI can reprioritize resources to other CIA functions.

There Is a Need for an Organization Dedicated to Unclassified Research and Analysis

When asked whether the open-source capabilities described above could be created within an existing agency, interview participants drew upon lessons from the past 15 years to conclude that any existing intelligence agency would treat OSINT as a lesser-included mission. However, their reasons for recommending that an organization dedicated to the collection and dissemination of OSINT should be independent were diverse and nuanced.

One interview participant stressed the importance of building transparency into the design of any organization charged with collecting PAI and producing OSINT analyses. If government leaders agree that open-source information is valuable and should be collected, then this foundation is built on an "uncomfortable truth," as one participant described it, that the American public would not be comfortable learning how intelligence agencies collect and use data—including data that would be available to themselves as citizens to purchase, if they chose. For this reason, an organization that collects open-source information could be designed with transparency built in—a feature that is certainly not inherent in CIA, the current home of OSE. This transparency would involve clear and public guidelines about how data are collected (e.g., through purchase agreements or other methods), processed (e.g., to ensure removal of personally identifiable information), and shared (e.g., perhaps including different rules for sharing with intelligence agencies versus law enforcement). Such transparency would not need to reveal the sources and methods themselves, only the guidelines applied. As a result, this organization would need a robust civil liberties division, a benefit that could centralize the legal disputes that interview participants described exist in various agencies.

Several interview participants speculated whether the United States would be better served if an open source–focused organization existed *outside* the IC. Such an organization would no longer be an *intelligence* organization but rather an *open-source research and analysis organization*, with a role and functions similar to those of the Congressional Research Service. The first benefit of such an organization would be its ability

---

[24] David C. Logan, "China's Nuclear Forces," testimony before the U.S.-China Economic and Security Review Commission, Washington, D.C., June 10, 2021.

to provide analytic products as a public service without the constraints of classification. This would allow the organization to provide assessments directly to the private sector and foreign partners who need access to them.

A second benefit of a nonintelligence research and analysis organization could be its capacity to serve as a kind of whole-of-government clearinghouse that would provide a place to aggregate information on data needs, data collection, and data use agreements. This organization could be tasked with developing policies and procedures articulating rules and guidelines for how data would be shared with environmental or agricultural agencies, intelligence agencies, law enforcement agencies, medical and health research agencies, and other users. Perceptions of government overreach would still be significant, and some of these concerns could be addressed through transparency and others through oversight, while others would likely remain.

A third potential benefit noted by some interview participants is that, if this new agency included large numbers of experts in "data tradecraft," it could provide the initial data processing to assess the credibility and gaps in data sets and provide context for agency users who lack sufficient numbers of skilled on-staff financial analysts, data scientists, translators, and other key personnel.

Several flaws in this model make it an interesting thought exercise even if it is not readily implementable. First, oversight of such an organization would be necessary. An inspector general could provide internal oversight, but the decision of which congressional committees would provide oversight would need to be determined. Second, this model could lead to the pitfall that we described earlier in which open-source information does not provide a full picture of the U.S. government's analysis on a topic, thus misleading users of the OSINT. Although this organization's products could be caveated for users, such caveats would not stop policymakers—in the U.S. government, in state and local governments, and in foreign governments—from acting on such information. By removing this organization from the IC, its products would no longer be presented as *intelligence* and could therefore be treated with similar credibility given to reputable journalism, i.e., that it is informative but only gives part of the full story. Lastly, such an organization would only be effective if it does not slow down access to data that organizations already have. If the organization were to become a bureaucratic bottleneck between users and the data that they are trying to access, then it will have failed.

This model could also prove challenging within the IC workforce. When all analysts are cleared at top secret levels, then everyone is competing for classified sources. If some analysts handled only unclassified information while others handled only classified information, the IC would have a two-tiered or caste system, which would create new problems without solving old ones, and uncleared analysts would risk being sidelined as "uninformed."

If, alternatively, there were an organization that relied solely on unclassified data and that organization produced unclassified analytic reporting, then those reports could be compared with classified all-source reports to identify (1) what gaps can only be closed with classified sources, (2) what analysis can be gleaned from solely unclassified sources and therefore could be shared with foreign partners or the public, and (3) which analytic topics could the IC answer with OSINT in order to focus other resources on topics about which OSINT is insufficient.

The ability to crowdsource the processing or analysis of open-source information (unofficially called "crowdsourced intelligence") was not mentioned by our interview participants, but it has been discussed elsewhere.[25] In *crowdsourced intelligence*, the public provides assistance on topics where the data are too voluminous and where machine learning solutions are not yet available. One example of this occurred in 2005, when the government released the Harmony database, which provided public access to documents recovered in Iraq in order to "contextualize the inner-functioning of al-Qa'ida, its associated movement, and

[25] Amy Zegart, "Spies Like Us: The Promise and Peril of Crowdsourced Intelligence," *Foreign Affairs*, July/August 2021b.

other security threats."[26] The most recent and most widely publicized example of crowdsourced intelligence was the identification of persons who trespassed and committed crimes in the U.S. Capitol Building on January 6, 2021.[27] Within days of the event, reports were already coming in from public "sleuths" processing large amounts of video and photos from that event, organizing these files by the severity of the crimes shown, and organizing the search for the identities of the perpetrators.

The FBI decided to ride this wave of public support by encouraging and soliciting the public's help in identifying the assailants.[28] When the Department of Justice began issuing arrest warrants and indictments based on crowdsourced identifications, those documents were accompanied by the government's own corroborating evidence, including witness statements, cell phone records, and other records. In other words, the use of crowdsourced intelligence still requires the government to apply its own verification of authenticity, but crowdsourcing can greatly reduce the size of the "haystack" (which on January 6, 2021, was 330 million Americans) that they have to search through to find the few important "needles" (the nearly 500 people arrested as of this writing).[29] Analysis of unclassified imagery is another topic that lends itself to crowdsourced intelligence, including imagery of human rights abuses,[30] humanitarian crises,[31] and illegal maritime activity.[32]

Despite the potential value of crowdsourced intelligence for the IC, one major hurdle remains: The IC is barred from tasking (or directing) nonemployees from conducting intelligence-gathering and is limited to "sensitizing" nongovernment individuals to IC information needs.[33] Therefore, if the government desires to create a crowdsourced analytic capability, one solution would be to place the management of this capability outside the IC—as a government-wide service rather than an intelligence function. If the government were to create an unclassified research and analysis organization outside the IC—rather than inside the IC—managing crowdsourcing is one function that it could conduct.

Nongovernmental Entities Are Engaging in National Security

So far, we have discussed findings related to current intelligence practice and the challenges in incorporating OSINT into intelligence assessments. Our interviews also highlighted a different kind of challenge for the IC, one that requires a broader understanding of U.S. national security threats. This requires acknowledging that the commercial sector, the academic and scientific research sector, and even private citizens are increasingly vulnerable to malign actions by individuals and foreign nation states seeking to exert their influence

---

[26] Combating Terrorism Center at West Point, "Harmony Program," webpage, undated.

[27] Greg Myre, "How Online Sleuths Identified Rioters at the Capitol," *NPR*, January 11, 2021.

[28] Amanda Macias, "FBI Requests Help from Public to Identify U.S. Capitol Rioters," CNBC, January 7, 2021.

[29] As of June 25, 2021, *USA Today* had reported that 487 people had been arrested, and the George Washington University Project on Extremism had tracked 499 federal cases (Dinah Pulver, Rachel Axon, Josh Salman, Katie Wedell, and Erin Mansfield, "Capitol Riot Arrests: See Who's Been Charged Across the U.S.," *USA Today*, June 22, 2021; GW Program on Extremism, "Capitol Hill Siege," webpage, undated). These numbers will likely continue to rise.

[30] David Hawk and Amanda Mortwedt Oh, *The Parallel Gulag: North Korea's 'An-Jeon-Bu' Prison Camps*, Washington, D.C.: Committee for Human Rights in North Korea, 2017.

[31] Shirley S. Wang, Newley Purnell, and Suryatapa Bhattacharya, "Nepal Aid Workers Helped by Drones, Crowdsourcing," *Wall Street Journal*, May 1, 2015.

[32] "Crowdsourcing to Spot Illegal Fishing Vessels at Cocos Island Marine Protected Area," *Earth Imaging Journal*, September 1, 2015.

[33] Executive Order 12333, 1981, as amended in 2008.

or undermine U.S. security using sophisticated cyber capabilities. When these foreign-sponsored operations occur on U.S. soil, the IC both lacks the mechanisms to partner with these U.S. entities at scale and lacks consensus that it is even within their mission to conduct intelligence assessments for entities outside the U.S. government. This section describes the "attack surface" of these foreign government operations, the role that nongovernmental entities are playing, and the need for intelligence-sharing with audiences outside the IC.

The "Attack Surface" for Foreign Threats Against the United States Increasingly Includes Civilian, Commercial, and Private Entities and Systems

The "attack surface" of foreign attacks against the United States increasingly involves nonmilitary targets, including physical targets, such as New York's World Trade Center towers, cyber targets, and even the "beliefs, attitudes, and behaviors" of ordinary Americans.[34] Russia conducted the most expensive cyberattack that the world has experienced to date, crippling global commercial supply chains.[35] North Korea perpetuated a ransomware attack against a movie studio to prevent the release of a film that disparaged its leader.[36] At least two of Apple's employees have been indicted for attempting to sell the firm's intellectual property to China, including schematics for autonomous vehicles.[37] And rather than hack voting machines, Russia decided to hack the voters themselves by conducting a covert influence campaign before the 2016 U.S. presidential election.[38]

One interview participant noted that the "threat surface is disproportionately outside government, and companies are making decisions that affect national security without us. . . . We've got to serve them." Another participant, citing 5G technology, asked, "How do we define national security interests?" Interview participants indicated that, even if intelligence exists to inform national security decisions, these decisions—such as those involving the development of 5G—are increasingly taking place in the commercial sector outside the halls of government. In such an environment where national security decisions—including decisions on how to respond to foreign disinformation, foreign technology transfer, and foreign cyber threats—are being made without government officials present, these decisions are also being made without the benefits of intelligence. The IC could choose to share intelligence with a wider audience for the benefit of national security, but it currently does not do so adequately.

The Private Sector Is Engaged in National Security, Whether the IC Wants to Acknowledge It or Not

The types of attacks described above as well as many other risks—pipeline attacks, ransomware, cyber vulnerabilities, technology transfer, joint venture partnerships in China, to name a few—indicate how the private sector is, by default, already engaged in national security, but without the benefit of receiving threat briefings or intelligence assessments about adversaries' intentions, strategies, and TTP. Private firms address

[34] Michael J. Mazarr, Ryan Michael Bauer, Abigail Casey, Sarah Anita Heintz, and Luke J. Matthews, *The Emerging Risk of Virtual Societal Warfare: Social Manipulation in a Changing Information Environment*, Santa Monica, Calif.: RAND Corporation, RR-2714-OSD, 2019.

[35] Andy Greenberg, "The Untold Story of Notpetya, the Most Devastating Cyberattack in History," *Wired*, August 22, 2018.

[36] Department of Justice, Office of Public Affairs, "North Korean Regime-Backed Programmer Charged with Conspiracy to Conduct Multiple Cyber Attacks and Intrusions," press release, Washington, D.C., September 6, 2018.

[37] Department of Justice, U.S. Attorney's Office, Northern District of California, "Former Apple Employee Indicted on Theft of Trade Secrets," press release, San Jose, Calif., July 16, 2018.

[38] ODNI, *Assessing Russian Activities and Intentions in Recent US Elections*, Intelligence Community Assessment, Washington, D.C., ICA 2017-01D, January 6, 2017.

different parts of this gap (more so in cybersecurity than in other threat sectors), but do so without access to classified sources, and many small businesses cannot afford or choose not to purchase these services, leaving these businesses uninformed and vulnerable.

Interview participants described a need to share information and *intelligence* with industry that is "relevant to the speed of decisionmaking" according to one participant. A foreign partner interview participant said that, when their country started sharing more information with industry, industry leaders began to better understand the government's stance toward China. Industry leaders did not want to lose out on business opportunities, but when they better understood the hidden risks of these deals, they became more aware of why the government was asking them to diversify away from China.

Interview participants suggested that the DNI could expand the IC's duty to warn by including these other types of threats. ICD 191 requires intelligence agencies to warn individuals of threats of violence—specifically threats of intentional killing, bodily harm, or kidnapping—even if the intended victims are not Americans. (The policy does not apply to persons who are terrorists or other nefarious actors.)[39] ICD 191 does not cite a statutory limitation that restricts this duty to acts of physical violence, and our research found no such limitation. Therefore, it would be within the DNI's authority to expand the duty to warn to other types of intelligence.

Limitations of Existing IC Statutes and Structures

In its report about the IC's ability to respond to China, HPSCI identified the IC's inability to fully integrate intelligence for many topic areas as one key finding. The report noted, "The Intelligence Community has failed to fully achieve the integration objectives outlined in the 2004 Intelligence Reform and Terrorism Prevention Act (IRTPA) for targets and topics unrelated to counterterrorism."[40] Our interviews revealed many ways in which limitations of existing IC statutes and structures affect the IC's ability to do its work. Here we focus on the statutory role of DNI, the delineation between foreign intelligence and domestic authorities, the structural design of the roles of Inspector General (IG) and Analytic Ombudsman, and the role and functions of DHS.

The Position of the DNI Has Not Achieved the Vision Imagined for It

For all the debate over the past 15 years over the DNI's role, one interview participant said that, during the Trump administration, "[it felt] like what we learned was that the DNI mattered." In other words, while DNI had played many roles over the years—consensus-builder, trusted advisor, portfolio manager, advocate for new programs—one takeaway from those four years was that the DNI's bureaucratic function may have been more useful than it is often given credit for. This participant explained that, in a healthy environment, the DNI creates a buffer between the intelligence agencies and the White House and the media, so that the agencies can focus on doing their jobs instead of being in the spotlight. However, under President Trump, when, according to this person, one of the DNIs considered himself responsible to the President rather than to the IC, this bureaucratic function was neglected, which left agencies to fend for themselves.

One challenge for any DNI is to serve as both a politically appointed Cabinet-level senior advisor and a nonpolitical intelligence professional. When the position of the DNI was created in 2004, it was given three principal responsibilities: (1) serve as head of the IC; (2) act as the principal adviser to the President, to the National Security Council, and to the Homeland Security Council for intelligence matters related to U.S.

---

[39] ICD 191, 2015.

[40] HPSCI, 2020, p. 27.

national security; and (3) oversee and direct the implementation of the National Intelligence Program.[41] However, when these first two responsibilities conflict with each other—that is, when a DNI is asked to choose between loyalty to the President and loyalty to the IC—a DNI cannot simultaneously act as the President's trusted intelligence advisor while also acting as the manager for the IC.

Some interview participants also suggested that the role of the DNI is both too broad and too weak. It is too broad because the first and second responsibilities described above require different skill sets, and one person is unlikely to excel at both, and it is too weak because the DNI lacks the budget authority that is implied in the position's third responsibility. One option suggested in our interviews is to make the DNI into a 10-year term similar to that of the FBI Director, so the DNI could tackle enduring changes that are not possible to address in a shorter term.

Adversaries Exploit U.S. Safeguards That Prevent Domestic Intelligence

Foreign threats or *foreign companies* are terms that, according to some interview participants, represent an antiquated mindset in today's environment. Foreign adversaries have demonstrated a willingness—and an eagerness—to co-opt U.S. citizens as influencers for their (disinformation) messaging and their (technology transfer) operations, and these countries exploit U.S. guardrails against domestic intelligence to do so. In the current environment, should a U.S. person who has been co-opted by a foreign government—either wittingly or unwittingly—be considered a "foreign threat" or a "domestic threat"? When intelligence on such activities contains no law enforcement nexus (i.e., no laws have been broken), the ability to understand and report on these threats is hindered by laws and regulations. Some interview participants acknowledged that many Americans prefer that their government has strong safeguards for civil liberties even at the risk of weakening U.S. national security, while other interview participants suggested that this is a "false choice." While serving as DNI, James Clapper addressed this challenge when he said, "We're also a people who—Constitutionally and culturally—attach a high premium to our personal freedoms and our personal privacy."[42]

Underlying this false choice is the notion that a free and democratic society cannot simultaneously have both domestic intelligence and freedom from governmental abuse of power. To identify lessons that may be replicable in the United States, we tested this notion by examining approaches that democratic allied governments use to conduct domestic intelligence.

The United Kingdom's Security Service (MI5) is subordinate to the UK Home Office, which is the government department responsible for immigration and passports, drug policy, crime, fire, counterterrorism, and police.[43] MI5 is an intelligence-gathering organization. It partners with national and county-level law enforcement organizations throughout the United Kingdom and, although MI5 itself has no law enforcement authority, provides evidence for law enforcement operations involved in deterrence and prosecution.[44] MI5 operates under a law called the Regulation of Investigatory Powers Act (RIPA), which spells out how and when domestic sources can legally provide information. Most relevant to this discussion, RIPA allows for the use of PAI.[45]

The Canadian Security Intelligence Service is Canada's principal national intelligence service. It is responsible for collecting, analyzing, and reporting intelligence on "threats to the security of Canada," regardless

---

[41] Public Law 108-458, Intelligence Reform and Terrorism Prevention Act of 2004, Sec. 1011, Reorganization and Improvement of Management of Intelligence Community, December 17, 2004.

[42] As quoted in ODNI, *Domestic Approach to National Intelligence*, Washington, D.C., NCTC 029197, December 2016, p. 6.

[43] Government of the United Kingdom, "Home Office: About Us," webpage, undated.

[44] UK Security Service, "MI5's Law and Governance," webpage, undated.

[45] Rachel Glover and Lyndsey Smith, *Regulation of Investigatory Powers: Policy and Procedure*, Basildon, United Kingdom: Basildon Council, June 3, 2019, p. 10.

of whether those threats are foreign or domestic.[46] It is responsible for conducting intelligence operations—clandestine and overt—at home and abroad. The Canadian Security Intelligence Service Act established the organization, and it explicitly forbids the Canadian Security Intelligence Service "from investigating acts of lawful advocacy, protest, or dissent."[47] It has no law enforcement authority, but it shares intelligence with the Royal Canadian Mounted Police.

In Germany, the Federal Office for the Protection of the Constitution (Bundesamt fuer Verfassungsschutz [BfV]) is the domestic intelligence service responsible for countering domestic threats, including counterterrorism and counterespionage. It operates under the Federal Ministry of the Interior, Building and Community and works closely with the foreign intelligence service (BND) and the military counterintelligence service (MAD). BfV has no law enforcement capabilities; it generally cannot collect information on individuals or collect personal information on German citizens unless it is authorized to do so by the law governing BfV operations and activities. Interestingly, in contrast to U.S. intelligence agencies, the BfV has a legal obligation to keep the German public informed and aware of possible threats to domestic security.[48]

We extracted several lessons from these countries' models for domestic intelligence. First, all three countries separate their intelligence functions from their law enforcement functions. In the United States, domestic intelligence is a function of the primary federal law enforcement organization, the FBI. Although this arrangement allows the FBI to use intelligence in support of criminal investigations, it also creates challenges that could possibly be overcome by separating the bureau's law enforcement and intelligence functions. Next, the other countries' models provided examples of two approaches that might be implementable in the United States: (1) the idea of legally requiring an intelligence agency to inform the public of threats to domestic security (Germany); and (2) creation of a legal authority for the collection of PAI (UK).

Deeper research on a larger number of countries could reveal a greater number of lessons for how the United States could shore up national security vulnerabilities that foreign adversaries exploit. One interview participant noted that a number of nations have developed new processes for managing evolving national security vulnerabilities. Estonia and Finland established public infrastructure to educate their respective populations on the dangers of foreign influence on public opinion and elections.[49] Other countries, such as Israel, have different approaches to domestic intelligence, and further study could reveal additional insights. We chose to limit research in this study to countries with similar cultural norms to those of the United States—the population's tolerance for domestic surveillance is strikingly different in Israel, for example—but further research could provide insights to inform future U.S. intelligence reforms.

Other Governments Have Different Intelligence Models That the United States Could Draw From

During our research, we learned about a different approach for organizing analytic oversight functions. Australia's Inspector General for Intelligence and Security (IGIS) provides independent assurance to ministers, the Parliament, and the public that the six Australian intelligence agencies under its jurisdiction are acting

---

[46] Government of Canada, "Canadian Security Intelligence Service," webpage, last updated October 26, 2021.

[47] Government of Canada, "Canadian Security Intelligence Service: Legislation," webpage, July 15, 2020b.

[48] Federal Ministry of the Interior, Building and Community, "Federal Office for the Protection of the Constitution," webpage, undated.

[49] Drew Springall, Travis Finkenauer, Zakir Durumeric, Jason Kitcat, Harri Hursti, Margaret MacAlpine, and J. Alex Halderman, "Security Analysis of the Estonian Internet Voting System," *CCS '14: Proceedings of the 2014 ACM SIGSAC Conference on Computer and Communications Security*, November 2014; Billy Perrigo, "Estonia Election: What the U.S. Can Learn About Electronic Voting from This Tiny Eastern European Nation," *Time*, March 1, 2019.

with legality, propriety, and consistency with human rights. To do this, IGIS undertakes a variety of investigations, considers complaints and public interest disclosures, and contributes to national security reviews and inquiries.[50] In comparison, in the U.S. intelligence system, the DNI's Analytic Ombudsman lacks the same protections and authorities as an IG, who is generally focused on fraud, waste, and abuse.[51] The IGIS conducts tradecraft audits on intelligence, has the authority to review any intelligence on any topic at any time, and provides reports directly to Cabinet ministers. Interestingly, in our research, we found that the Inspector General Act of 1978 describes the IG responsibilities as promoting the effectiveness of program administration,[52] which could reasonably be interpreted as the effectiveness of intelligence analysis. However, interview participants knew of no example of any IG exercising this authority over intelligence analysis and tradecraft. In the United States, such oversight would more likely be exercised by congressional intelligence oversight committees.

In Australia, anyone, including a member of the public, can go to the IGIS at any time to report a complaint, such as perceived politicization or pressure to change or water down an intelligence assessment, whereas in the United States, interview participants wondered where an intelligence officer would go with such a concern, especially if the concern originated within the officer's own chain of command. Although several IC agencies have an ombudsman, the DNI's Analytic Ombudsman is the only IC ombudsman with any statutory authority. All other agencies' ombudsmen are internally appointed positions with often unclear roles and responsibilities that can be changed at any time.

Similar to Australia's IGIS, Canada has an Intelligence Commissioner, who is responsible "for performing quasi-judicial reviews of the conclusions" on which decisions are made and drawn from intelligence.[53] The Intelligence Commissioner is a retired judge who serves part-time for a five-year term.[54] We did not conduct interviews with any Canadian officials; therefore, examining the strengths and limitations of the Office of the Intelligence Commissioner and identifying lessons about the office's successes since its creation in 2019 could be an area of further research.

However, creating an oversight role like an IGIS or Intelligence Commissioner within the U.S. executive branch—whether by expanding the role of an IG or the authorities of an ombudsman, or something else—would not prevent a malintentioned executive from leaving such a position vacant rather than risk inviting critical oversight. If the position were allowed to languish vacant, as many IG positions have for several years,[55] such a role would be of no value.

---

[50] Inspector-General of Intelligence and Security, "What We Do," webpage, undated.

[51] IRTPA required the DNI to "assign an individual or entity to be responsible for ensuring that finished intelligence products produced by any element or elements of the intelligence community are timely, objective, independent of political considerations, based upon all sources of available intelligence, and employ the standards of proper analytic tradecraft" (Pub. L. 108-458, Sec. 1019, Assignment of Responsibilities Relating to Analytic Integrity, 2004). This responsibility resides with the DNI's Analytic Ombudsman.

[52] Public Law 95-452, Inspector General Act of 1978, Sec. 2, Purpose and Establishment of Offices of Inspector General; Departments and Agencies Involved, October 12, 1978.

[53] Government of Canada, "Office of the Intelligence Commissioner: Raison d'Être, Mandate and Role: Who We Are and What We Do," webpage, March 6, 2020a.

[54] Government of Canada, "Intelligence Commissioner Act," webpage, June 21, 2019.

[55] Courtney Bublé, "More Than a Dozen IG Vacancies Await Nominees from Biden," *Government Executive*, March 11, 2021.

Some Intelligence Missions That Might Fall Under DHS Are Not Being Accomplished in Any Meaningful Way

ODNI describes DHS's intelligence responsibility in providing critical threat information to the entities that need it as follows: "DHS is responsible for the unified national effort to secure the U.S. by preventing and deterring terrorist attacks and responding to other threats and hazards. It also has statutory responsibilities to provide threat information to the owners and operators of critical infrastructure and key resources."[56]

Several interview participants mentioned the FBI and the State Department's Global Engagement Center as two ends of a spectrum in which the DHS Office of Intelligence and Analysis (I&A) could reasonably fill the middle ground, but it does not. In the current framework, the FBI provides law enforcement–focused threat information that can be used to open a case—either a criminal case, a terrorism case, or a counterintelligence case—or to begin a counterintelligence operation. Despite the FBI's assertions that it provides "threat intelligence," the overwhelming viewpoint outside the FBI is that investigative cases remain the metric used to measure all other measures at the FBI. At the other end of the spectrum, the Department of State's Global Engagement Center provides both domestic and global audiences with strategic intelligence on disinformation threats to the United States. The gap in the middle of these two ends, according to interview participants, is that no entity is taking strategic intelligence and making it actionable or useful to domestic audiences, nor is any organization taking tactical information—cyber threats, extremism threats, threats of intellectual property theft—and creating generalized intelligence assessments that could be used across industry sectors. Ideally, DHS would serve in that middle role.

This gap was evident on January 6, 2021. A 128-page Senate committee report about the security, planning, and response to that day's attack on the U.S. Capitol began by stating that both DHS and the FBI failed to issue intelligence threat assessments warning of the potential for violence, despite ample information publicly available online. The first page of the report states, "Despite online calls for violence at the Capitol, neither the FBI nor DHS issued a threat assessment or intelligence bulletin warning law enforcement entities in the National Capital Region of the potential for violence."[57]

Interview participants identified several examples of the types of intelligence that need to be provided to entities outside the government, including threat assessments, indicators, and threat vectors for domestic extremism; threat assessments that anticipate future cyber threats—new tactics and strategies—that may emerge months later; and threat assessments detailing risks from foreign talent programs. The State Department's Global Engagement Center has the mission to report on foreign disinformation campaigns in the United States, which is one threat area that overlaps with DHS's mission and where DHS could partner to create intelligence for U.S. consumers.

In a June 2021 article, the Center for American Progress described DHS's functions as follows:

> Despite consensus among policymakers that the department could be far more effective, there is little agreement on how to fix it. . . . it is time for DHS to focus on the missions and activities that it is uniquely capable of carrying out, and for which it, rather than other agencies, is the natural lead.[58]

The report continues, emphasizing the importance of communicating threat information to the American public and the role that DHS might play:

---

[56] ODNI, 2016.

[57] Committee on Homeland Security and Governmental Affairs and the Committee on Rules and Administration, 2021, p. 1.

[58] Mara Rudman, Rudy deLeon, Joel Martinez, Elisa Massimino, Silva Mathema, Katrina Mulligan, Alexandra Schmitt, and Philip E. Wolgin, "Redefining Homeland Security: A New Framework for DHS to Meet Today's Challenges," *Center for American Progress*, June 16, 2021.

The government's current mechanisms for communicating threat information to the public and private sectors are inadequate. In a world where the public and private sectors must take independent action to ensure America's safety and security, the government needs a trusted, effective mechanism to communicate threat information, including intelligence information, with the public and private sectors and between different levels of state, local, and federal government officials. Without such a mechanism, America lacks critical information on threats that could be mitigated, and the government is unable to enlist the capacity of American businesses and the American people in its threat response. DHS already plays an important role connecting federal entities and officials to their state, local, tribal, and territorial counterparts and has had success coordinating security and resilience efforts across the private and public sectors through Joint Terrorism Task Forces and other mechanisms. But there is no agency that currently leads the federal government's efforts at the national level to share information, advocate for greater government transparency, or develop new communications capacities that add value to the American people.[59]

Discussions about improving the effectiveness of intelligence to U.S. audiences outside government led to discussions about domestic intelligence. A few interview participants were open to the idea of revisiting U.S. limitations on domestic intelligence. One person said that the United States has "perverted the missions of DHS and FBI" because neither organization is designed or organized to provide the type of threat intelligence that is needed today, but no one else is authorized to do it either. This interview participant suggested that solving this problem ended up on "the cutting room floor" after the reports of the WMD and 9/11 Commissions came out because finding solutions was considered "too high of a mountain to climb."

One option to address this issue that we heard during interviews is to create a mechanism in which assessments developed by nongovernmental entities—such as private intelligence firms, academic researchers, or nongovernmental organizations—could be shared by the U.S. government. Perhaps if a government entity had tradecraft standards for reviewing nongovernmental research, it could provide assurance that specific products meet those standards.

The Politicization of Intelligence

The politicization of intelligence was a topic that came up frequently during our interviews, and it is a topic that has been discussed in many other forums as well. In a letter to the SSCI, Barry Zulauf, the DNI's Analytic Ombudsman, wrote, "Politicization need not be overt to be felt."[60] In an era where one person's fact is another person's fake news—or "alternative fact"—the leaders whom we interviewed described the changing political environment and political discourse seeping into the IC in ways that they had not anticipated, and they suggested that the IC is ill prepared to respond effectively to them. Our study did not comprehensively examine politicization in intelligence. Rather, this was one of many topic areas that was raised in the course of our research, and the sheer frequency with which it was raised led to its inclusion as a category of our findings. This section discusses four findings about politicization that arose during our interviews.

Politicization Is Hard to Define, but Often Recognizable When It Occurs
Given the often very different goals of intelligence analysts and policymakers, the politicization of intelligence has long been a concern. In James C. Thomson's 1968 article in *The Atlantic*, "How Could Vietnam

[59] Rudman et al., 2021.

[60] Barry A. Zulauf, IC Analytic Ombudsman, Office of the Director of National Intelligence, "Independent IC Analytic Ombudsman's on Politicization of Intelligence," letter to the U.S. Senate Select Committee on Intelligence, Washington, D.C., January 6, 2021, p. 8.

Happen? An Autopsy," he criticized, among other things, the lack of analytic thinking in government and the banishment of expertise. Thomson had served on the National Security Council under President Johnson until he resigned in protest of the Vietnam War. He asked, "Where were the experts, the doubters, and the dissenters?" and he answered his own question, saying that "real expertise" was replaced with "[t]he frantic skimming of briefing papers in the back seats of limousines" and "internal doubters and dissenters did indeed appear and persist," but they were *domesticated*.[61] "Domestication," he said, occurred when dissent was welcomed in civilized meetings: The dissenter feels proud to have spoken up, while the other participants in the room can feel satisfied that they allowed dissent to happen.[62] All is well, and business can proceed—except, of course, all was most certainly not well. From Vietnam to September 11, 2001, to present day, politicization has made analysts wary to present analysis that is "not compatible with the goals of policymakers."[63] One can only imagine what Thomson would say today of policymakers relying on tweets for news or intelligence officers publishing infographics in the President's Daily Brief (PDB).[64]

One interview participant described modern politicization as being difficult to define, but clearly present nonetheless:

> Politicization is an often-used word. In my experience, [I'm] not sure what it means these days. Everyone politicizes everything. None of those lepers had longer fingers than the next one. Administration, Congress, Democrats, Republicans, media pours gas on everything, and I would not have believed it two years ago, and [I would have] told you that politicization wasn't a thing inside the IC, but it is. It's not surprising given the ionized political environment that some [of that politicization] would bleed in, because it did.

Zulauf described the politicization challenge that the IC was facing in a letter to the Senate intelligence committee:

> Top ODNI officials faced enormous pressure to balance between IC assessments and customers' demands. This pressure filtered back down the chain and analysts perceived their work as being politicized, in contravention to the Analytic Standards for Objectivity and avoiding political considerations, in order to make intelligence more palatable to senior customers. Their response to the perceived—and sometimes real—attempts at politicization reflected a loss of analytic objectivity. When analysts face perceived politicization, they have recourse to report their concerns to the Ombudsman just as they have the obligation to continue to produce timely, accurate, objective intelligence with no regard for political considerations.[65]

Some interview participants in this study may agree with Thomson and Zulauf; they also offered their own concerns about the politicization of intelligence. One participant said,

> Obviously, there is political influence and always has been. It went to a dark and unnecessary place over the last couple of years. Part of the issue with dealing with foreign malign influence was making it look like you *weren't* being political, and how that played out in the China community and Russia community, and they both took wildly different approaches.

---

[61] James C. Thomson, "How Could Vietnam Happen? An Autopsy," *The Atlantic*, April 1968.

[62] Thomson, 1968.

[63] Carmen A. Medina, "What to Do When Traditional Models Fail," *Studies in Intelligence*, Vol. 46, No. 3, 2002, p. 9; John A. Gentry, "A New Form of Politicization? Has the CIA Become Institutionally Biased or Politicized?" *International Journal of Intelligence and CounterIntelligence*, Vol. 31, No. 4, 2018.

[64] The *PDB* is the term for the daily intelligence briefing provided to dozens of senior government officials. In this context, the term is not referring to the briefing given solely to the President.

[65] Zulauf, 2021, p. 8.

Decisions about which intelligence to include or not include in the PDB took on new political weight; multiple interview participants described analysts omitting the words "climate change" from intelligence assessments (an omission that carried over to the PDB) while other analysts insisted that intelligence on Russia should be included in the PDB, even when there were no new analytic judgments of substance.

The decision to hold the DNI's annual threat assessment briefing before an unclassified session of Congress was not previously a political decision before 2019. That year, President Trump berated intelligence leaders on Twitter over his disagreements with their assessments of Iran's nuclear program and the Islamic State.[66] After that, the DNI stopped offering unclassified intelligence briefings to Congress, instead opting for classified-only briefings, until 2021 when the unclassified briefings resumed. Although the decision to provide classified-only briefings may have allowed Congress to continue receiving intelligence, it prevented the American public from receiving intelligence from government officials who were not peddling overt political agendas.

Although senior intelligence officers walk the tightrope between trying to be perceived as nonpolitical and trying to *actually be* nonpolitical, some interview participants suggested that the media was driving a wedge through these issues. When the media latched onto any reports of conflict between the IC and the White House, for example, such reports created or exasperated the very conflict that intelligence officers were striving to overcome with their policy customers.

One interview participant explained that, during this era, the *ethics* of intelligence was the foundational cornerstone that the intelligence profession could have—and should have—rested on. In this person's experience, it is ethics—not tradecraft or TTP—that explains why customers come to the IC instead of getting their information elsewhere.

"Everyone Is a Political Hack, Except Me"

Several interview participants noted that people tend to see political bias in others—but not in themselves. Those who have served at the highest levels of the U.S. executive branch and within the U.S. legislative branch said that *political* is the term levied on anyone who takes an opposing viewpoint to one's own. By this definition, each individual is judge and jury to everyone else's political bias. One interview participant described congressional politicking as, "One side thinks something is politicized, the other side thinks it's factually accurate. Debate over politicization of intelligence depends on who's using [the intelligence] and who's politicizing it." When every elected official is a politician, there is no agreement about what constitutes *politicization*. Someone said, "If I'm [a lawmaker who is] asking questions about domestic extremism, am I doing responsible oversight to make sure you're doing everything to examine it, or am I a political hack who's trying to embarrass the previous President?" Avoiding politicization—by applying only good intentions when using intelligence—becomes an individual responsibility and is therefore impossible to regulate.

This take on politicization also puts a new spin on Henry Kissinger's famous adage: "You warned me, but you did not persuade me."[67] If the politician chooses to not be warned, then what role should the intelligence officer take? For example, one interview participant said that, after reviewing the evidence, their conclusion was that the COVID-19 pandemic was not an intelligence failure. This person said they "saw the reports, the IC was doing its job, and the customer set was not receptive." This person then asked, "How many times should the IC tell the customer something if the customer doesn't want to hear it?"

[66] Caitlin Oprysko, "Trump Tells Intel Chiefs to 'Go Back to School' After They Break with Him," *Politico*, January 30, 2019.

[67] Henry Kissinger, as quoted in Roger Z. George and James B. Bruce, eds., *Analyzing Intelligence: Origins, Obstacles, and Innovations*, Washington, D.C.: Georgetown University Press, 2008, p. 113.

Another interview participant described how their organization's intelligence on Russia and China was being compared with viewpoints that customers already held: "[the intelligence] annoyed the hard liners who wanted to beat up China at all costs, and it annoyed the ones who wanted to invest in China at all costs, so I guess we got it right." By this metric, the only insulation against politicization is to provide intelligence that disappoints all customers, or an intelligence version of "good people on both sides."

When intelligence officers choose which topics to publish and disseminate based on what they *want* their customers to hear, one interview participant said the result is that "we're not even aware of how we're actually biased ourselves."

Intelligence Officers Who Perceive Political Bias in Others May Institute Their Own Biased Remedies

For many intelligence officers, the response to perceived politicization—the perception that one's intelligence is being politicized, that an intelligence officer is being personally accused of being political, or that the customer is being biased—was to institute their own remedies, which, arguably, were in some cases as bad as the disease. Two such "remedies" included not sharing with customers intelligence that officers feared would be misused and trying to *shape* the policymaker's thinking, rather than simply *informing* it.

When intelligence officers attempted to avoid politicization *too strongly*, at least one interview participant described these officers as erring on the side of producing intelligence that was not useful. Rather than inform policy, these officers took a stand of only reporting information for which they had 99-percent certainty, which was not useful to any consumers. This tendency has existed in the IC for many years, and analysts have doubled down on this behavior more recently. The viewpoint is that, after the IC got the Iraq National Intelligence Estimate so wrong,[68] analysts stopped reporting on intelligence that had less than "98-percent certainty," and, in this person's opinion, "98-percent certainty is not intelligence" but rather news reporting.

An interview participant said that, when analysts bend over backward not to influence policy, they make themselves irrelevant to decisionmakers. When analysts avoid discussions that may lead to decisions about handling terrorists or what should be done about 5G—two examples raised in interviews—decisions are made without the benefit of intelligence. Senior government officials do not stop making decisions simply because intelligence officers have extracted themselves from the discussion; rather, they make decisions that are not informed by intelligence.

Meanwhile, another interview participant placed the blame on analytic managers, saying, "[the] real issue that analytic managers had was that they were so worried about a charge of politicization that they didn't do their job in the middle. . . . Analysts were not trained how to deal with the politically charged environment. [Tradecraft] standards won't help deal with it." Structures and guardrails that reduce, prevent, or mitigate political bias and other forms of bias from influencing intelligence outputs help to counter an individual's belief that they need to create their own remediations. The next finding offers one such possible approach.

Intelligence Professionals Lack Training to Address the Challenges of Politicization

Those intelligence professionals who reach the pinnacles of intelligence careers face situations for which none of their previous training or experiences have prepared them, and there is no playbook or training class to provide guidance. Interview participants described situations that they themselves were ill-prepared for—situations that no training course covers or, in their opinion, could cover, because each situation was so

---

[68] National Public Radio, "Michael Hayden: Blame Intel Agencies, Not White House, for Getting Iraq Wrong," *All Things Considered*, February 22, 2016.

nuanced. One interview participant suggested that perhaps if they had participated in discussion seminars or quarterly discussion groups where senior officials could come together and discuss case studies, such a venue would have allowed shared learning. Another participant said that military officers get training on how *not* to follow an unlawful order, but what training should a senior intelligence officer receive about how to assess whether a policymaker is asking a question with genuine interest or trying to embarrass a political leader of the opposing party?

Suggestions for training proposed by interview participants included the following:

- training for senior officials newly entering the senior executive service ranks to better understand the National Security Council and senior executive branch customers
- media training about the nuances of how the media will use intelligence and how senior IC leaders should consider this in their decisions about declassifying assessments or preparing for congressional testimony
- training on how to decide which topics should be chosen for the PDB and how often the same topic should be chosen so as not to give disproportionate weight to some topics over others.

One interview participant referred to a *War on the Rocks* article just before our interview began. In this article, a military lawyer described the burden that he carried of having to decide whether a planned military operation was legal or illegal—but never whether it was the right or moral thing to do. The lawyer described "working hard to ingratiate myself, to be seen by teammates as something other than a naysayer, to identify solutions and not just problems."[69] He described the pressure to approve an operation, but noted that, if he said no, a great deal of other people's work and planning would be for naught. Our interview participant described similar pressures on the intelligence analyst to look at not only one alternative but all possible alternatives, even if they were implausible or unreasonable. Otherwise, they continued, the analyst runs the risk of being accused of being a poor analyst even if considering such alternatives gives credibility to options that ought not be given credibility.

Another area suggested for new training concerns the ethics of intelligence. If ethics provide the foundation for the credibility of intelligence, then participants described a dearth of training on intelligence ethics. Compared with the medical or legal professions—which have annual ethics training requirements—an interview participant said, "We actually spend very little time teaching our people about intelligence ethics."

When analysts accuse their managers of "watering down" their assessments, when managers defend their actions as having removed weaker judgments not supported by the intelligence, and when the PDB team chooses not to include that assessment in the daily briefing, each of these decisions can be described either as politicization or as defending the IC against politicizing intelligence. Training analysts, managers, and senior officials on these different roles, the mechanics of how and why these decisions are made, and the context for these decisions would provide an important remedy against a loss of objectivity.

Chapter Conclusion

Our two Big Ideas were informed by the findings presented in this chapter. However, not all of these findings are directly associated with these Big Ideas: Several findings will require more in-depth research and analysis and will need to be informed by additional discussion with different stakeholders. We included all the findings in this chapter because we do not know which observations may provide a useful direction in a future

---

[69] E. M. Liddick, "No Legal Objection, Per Se," *War on the Rocks*, April 21, 2021.

crisis and because we hope that the full range of findings will inspire additional thought and research. In the concluding chapter, we provide some ideas for future exploration.

CHAPTER FOUR

Conclusion

This study was not designed to focus on OSINT, but as we asked one interview participant after another how to overcome politicization (sunlight is the best disinfectant), how to monitor foreign adversary activities in the United States (use open sources), and how to reveal these activities to affected Americans and commercial entities (release intelligence publicly), all roads led to OSINT. Other changes are needed too, but what we learned is that *substantive* change for the IC does not require major overhaul and reform. Interview participants repeatedly stated that any existing intelligence agency would treat OSINT as a lesser-included mission, and that OSINT needs a functional manager and dedicated organization in order to thrive. Insights from these interviews and other findings from our research have led us to propose two Big Ideas to support intelligence reform:

- **Create a new organization responsible for unclassified data (collection) and open-source intelligence (analysis).** This new organization would be designed to overcome some of the most-stubborn hurdles preventing OSINT from being more widely used today. It would establish a functional manager for OSINT, and this functional manager would be independent of any other functional manager. Such a significant policy and organizational change would allow an OSINT workforce to develop tradecraft, collect PAI, and produce OSINT products without the tangible or demoralizing effects of being deprioritized by a parent organization that prioritizes other disciplines. Meanwhile, this new organization could be designed with the deliberate goal of providing OSINT across intelligence support to defense missions, national intelligence missions, homeland security missions, and law enforcement missions. This change could enable the IC to better monitor foreign disinformation campaigns and to incorporate more effectively Chinese government planning and strategy documents into its all-source analysis.
- **Provide intelligence as a service to the American public.** This would be a major leap forward in the IC to acknowledge that the attack surface for national security threats is increasingly nongovernmental and that the leaders who must decide how to respond to these threats are often uninformed by intelligence. The policy change that we recommend would allow the DNI to signal to the commercial and nongovernmental sectors that the IC is attempting to address their plight as the targets of attacks from foreign governments and other foreign actors while signaling to intelligence analysts that they are empowered to nominate all-source analytic products that should be submitted for public release approval or for release to specific sectors or entities. As products are submitted for release approval and as the analytic review process addresses these threats on a case-by-case basis, the IC would begin to establish processes that may be scaled later into repeatable mechanisms.

These game-changing ideas are bold and audacious but also implementable right now.

Ideas for Further Research and Discussion

Several ideas embedded in this report's findings would benefit from further research and discussion. We lacked the resources to dive deep enough into these issues to provide the fuller examination that they deserve. We present these ideas here because they are worthy of further examination:

- **If not already completed or underway, the IC should engage in a pilot test case to improve intelligence-sharing between the IC and the private sector on cyber threats.** Such a narrow topic area would enable the IC to develop new policies and mechanisms to use in disseminating threat assessments, including forward-looking trend forecasts, to the private sector with sources removed. The policies and mechanisms that work in this test case could be scaled beyond cyber across all other types of threats and topics.
- **Create mechanisms for a government organization to apply analytic tradecraft standards to assessments developed by nongovernmental entities—such as private intelligence firms, academic researchers, or nongovernmental organizations—so these assessments could be shared by the U.S. government with wider public audiences.** An IC "stamp of approval" for nongovernmental analyses that meet analytic tradecraft standards would create a force multiplier for the IC, allowing it to provide more unclassified assessments than it can produce within its own budget and on topics where the IC's expertise might be weaker than other sectors' expertise (such as cybersecurity or topics requiring language skills that are lacking in the IC). The IC could begin this with a few products per year to indicate that they do not intend to review all products produced.
- **Identify a list of intelligence topics that are routinely conducted in classified all-source products and test how well OSINT analysts could cover the same topics.** If OSINT analysis reaches the same analytic conclusions as the all-source analysis, perhaps these topics can be covered either by OSINT or by outside researchers, with occasional classified collection used to verify whether changes to the baseline analysis have occurred. This would free up valuable resources to enable exquisite collection to be tasked to other targets.
- **Examine options for how the U.S. government could facilitate crowdsourcing, whether within the IC or as a government service conducted by a non-IC entity.** The attack against the Capitol on January 6, 2021, offers a case study for the government's use of crowdsourcing, and the government can examine how to capture the lessons learned and develop options for implementing a repeatable approach.
- **Research options for alternative approaches to domestic intelligence that would be legal under the U.S. Constitution and adhere to U.S. cultural values while overcoming the challenges of the IC's current system.** This study could include an examination of the legal frameworks in the United States, an examination of other democracies' legal frameworks and organizational structures, and a review of options for improving DHS's intelligence functions.

Closing Thoughts

The IC has a critical role to play in protecting national security. But the current environment demands prompt examination and consideration of changes to intelligence structures and authorities to ensure that intelligence analysts can do their jobs effectively. Our aim in proposing these two Big Ideas, along with our other findings and ideas for further research and discussion, is to help illuminate that meaningful change within the IC is well within reach.

Abbreviations

BfV	Bundesamt fuer Verfassungsschutz [Federal Office for the Protection of the Constitution (Germany)]
CIA	Central Intelligence Agency
COVID-19	coronavirus disease 2019
CSIS	Canadian Security Intelligence Service
DHS	Department of Homeland Security
DIA	Defense Intelligence Agency
DNI	Director of National Intelligence
FBI	Federal Bureau of Investigation
GEOINT	geospatial intelligence
HPSCI	House Permanent Select Committee on Intelligence (a.k.a. House Intelligence Committee)
HUMINT	human intelligence
I&A	Office of Intelligence and Analysis (part of DHS)
IC	intelligence community
ICD	Intelligence Community Directive
IG	Inspector General
IGIS	Inspector General for Intelligence and Security (in Australia)
INT	intelligence discipline
IRTPA	Intelligence Reform and Terrorism Prevention Act
ODNI	Office of the Director of National Intelligence
OSE	Open Source Enterprise
OSINT	open-source intelligence
PAI	publicly available information
PDB	President's Daily Brief
SIGINT	signals intelligence
SSCI	Senate Select Committee on Intelligence
TTP	tactics, techniques, and procedures

USCC   U.S.-China Economic and Security Review Commission

WMD Commission   Commission on the Intelligence Capabilities of the United States Regarding Weapons of Mass Destruction

References

Brown, Zachery Tyson, and Carmen A. Medina, "The Declining Market for Secrets," *Foreign Affairs*, March 9, 2021.

Bublé, Courtney, "More Than a Dozen IG Vacancies Await Nominees from Biden," *Government Executive*, March 11, 2021.

Castro, Joaquin, "Congressman Castro Introduces Bipartisan Bill to Create China and Russian Translation and Analysis Center," press release, Washington, D.C., July 28, 2021.

Central Intelligence Agency, "About CIA," webpage, undated. As of June 24, 2021:
https://www.cia.gov/about/

CIA—*See* Central Intelligence Agency.

Combating Terrorism Center at West Point, "Harmony Program," webpage, undated. As of July 12, 2021:
https://ctc.usma.edu/harmony-program/

Committee on Homeland Security and Governmental Affairs and the Committee on Rules and Administration, *Examining the U.S. Capitol Attack: A Review of the Security, Planning, and Response Failures on January 6*, staff report, Washington, D.C.: U.S. Senate, June 8, 2021.

"Crowdsourcing to Spot Illegal Fishing Vessels at Cocos Island Marine Protected Area," *Earth Imaging Journal*, September 1, 2015.

Davitch, James M., "Open Sources for the Information Age: Or How I Learned to Stop Worrying and Love Unclassified Data," *Joint Force Quarterly*, Vol. 87, 4th Quarter, October 2017, pp. 18–25.

Department of Justice, Office of Public Affairs, "North Korean Regime-Backed Programmer Charged with Conspiracy to Conduct Multiple Cyber Attacks and Intrusions," press release, Washington, D.C., September 6, 2018.

Department of Justice, U.S. Attorney's Office, Northern District of California, "Former Apple Employee Indicted on Theft of Trade Secrets," press release, San Jose, Calif., July 16, 2018.

Durbin, Brent, *The CIA and the Politics of US Intelligence Reform*, Cambridge, United Kingdom: Cambridge University Press, 2017.

Ellehuus, Rachel, and Donatienne Ruy, "Did Russia Influence Brexit?" *Center for Strategic and International Studies*, July 21, 2020.

Evanina, William, "Threat Briefing," in *China Initiative Conference*, video, Center for Strategic and International Studies, February 6, 2020. As of January 20, 2021:
https://www.csis.org/events/china-initiative-conference

Executive Order 12333, *United States Intelligence Activities*, December 4, 1981, as amended by Executive Orders 13284 (2003), 13355 (2004), and 13470 (2008).

FBI—*See* Federal Bureau of Investigation.

Federal Bureau of Investigation, *Executive Summary—China: The Risk to Corporate America*, Washington, D.C., undated.

Federal Ministry of the Interior, Building and Community, "Federal Office for the Protection of the Constitution," webpage, undated. As of July 26, 2021:
https://www.bmi.bund.de/EN/topics/security/protection-of-the-constitution/
protection-of-the-constitution.html

Gartin, Joseph W., "The Future of Analysis," *Studies in Intelligence*, Vol. 63, No. 2, June 2019, pp. 1–5.

Gentry, John A., "A New Form of Politicization? Has the CIA Become Institutionally Biased or Politicized?" *International Journal of Intelligence and CounterIntelligence*, Vol. 31, No. 4, 2018, pp. 647–680.

George, Roger Z., and James B. Bruce, eds., *Analyzing Intelligence: Origins, Obstacles, and Innovations*, Washington, D.C.: Georgetown University Press, 2008.

Glasser, Susan B., "Ex-Spy Chief: Russia's Election Hacking Was an 'Intelligence Failure,'" *Global Politico*, podcast transcript, December 11, 2017. As of June 18, 2021:
https://www.politico.eu/article/ex-spy-chief-russias-election-hacking-was-an-intelligence-failure/

Global Engagement Center, *GEC Special Report: Pillars of Russia's Disinformation and Propaganda Ecosystem*, Washington, D.C.: U.S. Department of State, August 2020.

Glover, Rachel, and Lyndsey Smith, *Regulation of Investigatory Powers: Policy and Procedure*, Basildon, United Kingdom: Basildon Council, June 3, 2019.

Government of Canada, "Intelligence Commissioner Act," webpage, June 21, 2019. As of July 26, 2021:
https://laws-lois.justice.gc.ca/eng/acts/I-14.85/page-1.html

———, "Office of the Intelligence Commissioner: Raison d'Être, Mandate and Role: Who We Are and What We Do," webpage, March 6, 2020a. As of July 26, 2021:
https://www.canada.ca/en/intelligence-commissioner/raisondetre-mandate-and-role.html

———, "Canadian Security Intelligence Service: Legislation," webpage, July 15, 2020b. As of July 26, 2021:
https://www.canada.ca/en/security-intelligence-service/corporate/legislation.html

———, "Canadian Security Intelligence Service," webpage, last updated October 26, 2021. As of July 26, 2021:
https://www.canada.ca/en/security-intelligence-service.html

Government of the United Kingdom, "Home Office: About Us," webpage, undated. As of July 26, 2021:
https://www.gov.uk/government/organisations/home-office/about

Greenberg, Andy, "The Untold Story of NotPetya, the Most Devastating Cyberattack in History," *Wired*, August 22, 2018, pp. 52–63.

GW Program on Extremism, "Capitol Hill Siege," webpage, undated. As of June 25, 2021:
https://extremism.gwu.edu/Capitol-Hill-Cases

Hamel, Liz, Lunna Lopes, Grace Sparks, Mellisha Stokes, and Mollyann Brodie, "KFF COVID-19 Vaccine Monitor: April 2021," polling findings, Kaiser Family Foundation, May 6, 2021. As of June 18, 2021:
https://www.kff.org/coronavirus-covid-19/poll-finding/kff-covid-19-vaccine-monitor-april-2021/

Hastedt, Glenn, "The Schlesinger Report: Its Place in Past, Present and Future Studies of Improving Intelligence Analysis," *Intelligence and National Security,* Vol. 24, No. 3, 2009, pp. 422–428.

Hawk, David, and Amanda Mortwedt Oh, *The Parallel Gulag: North Korea's 'An-Jeon-Bu' Prison Camps*, Washington, D.C.: Committee for Human Rights in North Korea, 2017.

Hitchens, Theresa, "New Strategy Aims to Up DoD, IC Game to Counter Disinformation," *Breaking Defense*, March 16, 2021.

House Permanent Select Committee on Intelligence, *IC21: The Intelligence Community in the 21st Century*, staff study, Washington, D.C.: U.S. Government Printing Office, 1996.

———, *The China Deep Dive: A Report on the Intelligence Community's Capabilities and Competencies with Respect to the People's Republic of China*, unclassified executive summary, Washington, D.C., September 2020.

HPSCI—*See* House Permanent Select Committee on Intelligence.

ICD—*See* Intelligence Community Directive.

Inspector-General of Intelligence and Security, "What We Do," webpage, undated. As of August 31, 2021:
https://www.igis.gov.au/what-we-do

Intelligence Community Directive 203, *Analytic Standards*, Washington, D.C.: Office of the Director of National Intelligence, January 2, 2015.

Intelligence Community Directive 191, *Duty to Warn*, Washington, D.C.: Office of the Director of National Intelligence, July 21, 2015.

Jontz, Sandra, "The Intelligence Everyone Can See," *SIGNAL*, September 1, 2017.

Katz, Brian, "The Collection Edge: Harnessing Emerging Technologies for Intelligence Collection," CSIS Brief, Washington, D.C.: Center for Strategic and International Studies, July 2020.

Kent, Sherman, *Strategic Intelligence for American World Policy*, Princeton, N.J.: Princeton University Press, 1966.

Liddick, E. M., "No Legal Objection, Per Se," *War on the Rocks*, April 21, 2021.

Logan, David C., "China's Nuclear Forces," testimony before the U.S.-China Economic and Security Review Commission, Washington, D.C., June 10, 2021.

Macias, Amanda, "FBI Requests Help from Public to Identify U.S. Capitol Rioters," CNBC, January 7, 2021.

Marcellino, William, Christian Johnson, Marek N. Posard, and Todd C. Helmus, *Foreign Interference in the 2020 Election: Tools for Detecting Online Election Interference*, Santa Monica, Calif.: RAND Corporation, RR-A704-2, 2020. As of June 18, 2021:
https://www.rand.org/pubs/research_reports/RRA704-2.html

Matthews, Miriam, Katya Migacheva, and Ryan Andrew Brown, *Superspreaders of Malign and Subversive Information on COVID-19: Russian and Chinese Efforts Targeting the United States*, Santa Monica, Calif.: RAND Corporation, RR-A112-11, 2021. As of June 15, 2021:
https://www.rand.org/pubs/research_reports/RRA112-11.html

Mazarr, Michael J., Ryan Michael Bauer, Abigail Casey, Sarah Anita Heintz, and Luke J. Matthews, *The Emerging Risk of Virtual Societal Warfare: Social Manipulation in a Changing Information Environment*, Santa Monica, Calif.: RAND Corporation, RR-2714-OSD, 2019. As of December 1, 2021:
https://www.rand.org/pubs/research_reports/RR2714.html

Medina, Carmen A., "What to Do When Traditional Models Fail," *Studies in Intelligence,* Vol. 46, No. 3, 2002, pp. 23–28.

Myre, Greg, "How Online Sleuths Identified Rioters at the Capitol," *NPR*, January 11, 2021.

National Public Radio, "Michael Hayden: Blame Intel Agencies, Not White House, for Getting Iraq Wrong," *All Things Considered*, February 22, 2016.

ODNI—*See* Office of the Director of National Intelligence.

Office of the Director of National Intelligence, "Objectivity," webpage, undated. As of July 12, 2021:
https://www.dni.gov/index.php/how-we-work/objectivity

———, *Domestic Approach to National Intelligence*, Washington, D.C., NCTC 029197, December 2016.

———, *Assessing Russian Activities and Intentions in Recent US Elections*, Intelligence Community Assessment, Washington, D.C., ICA 2017-01D, January 6, 2017.

———, "Background to 'Assessing Russian Activities and Intentions in Recent US Elections': The Analytic Process and Cyber Incident Attribution," in ODNI, 2017.

Oprysko, Caitlin, "Trump Tells Intel Chiefs to 'Go Back to School' After They Break with Him," *Politico*, January 30, 2019.

Perrigo, Billy, "Estonia Election: What the U.S. Can Learn About Electronic Voting from This Tiny Eastern European Nation," *Time*, March 1, 2019.

Pincus, Walter, "Ex-CIA Official Faults Use of Data on Iraq; Intelligence 'Misused' to Justify War, He Says," *Washington Post*, February 10, 2006.

Posard, Marek N., Marta Kepe, Hilary Reininger, James V. Marrone, Todd C. Helmus, and Jordan R. Reimer, *From Consensus to Conflict: Understanding Foreign Measures Targeting U.S. Elections*, Santa Monica, Calif.: RAND Corporation, RR-A704-1, 2020. As of June 18, 2021:
https://www.rand.org/pubs/research_reports/RRA704-1.html

Public Law 95-452, Inspector General Act of 1978, October 12, 1978.

Public Law 108-458, Intelligence Reform and Terrorism Prevention Act of 2004, December 17, 2004.

Pulver, Dinah, Rachel Axon, Josh Salman, Katie Wedell, and Erin Mansfield, "Capitol Riot Arrests: See Who's Been Charged Across the U.S.," *USA Today*, June 22, 2021. As of June 25, 2021:
https://www.usatoday.com/storytelling/capitol-riot-mob-arrests/

Rudman, Mara, Rudy deLeon, Joel Martinez, Elisa Massimino, Silva Mathema, Katrina Mulligan, Alexandra Schmitt, and Philip E. Wolgin, "Redefining Homeland Security: A New Framework for DHS to Meet Today's Challenges," *Center for American Progress*, June 16, 2021.

Select Committee on Intelligence, *Report of the Select Committee on Intelligence, United States Senate, on Russian Active Measures Campaigns and Interference in the 2016 U.S. Election, Vol. 1: Russian Efforts Against Election Infrastructure with Additional Views*, 116th Congress, redacted report, Washington, D.C., date redacted.

Silberman, Laurence H., Charles S. Robb, Richard C. Levin, John McCain, Henry S. Rowen, Walter B. Slocombe, William O. Studeman, Patricia M. Wald, Charles M. Vest, and Lloyd Cutler, *The Commission on the Intelligence Capabilities of the United States Regarding Weapons of Mass Destruction: Report to the President of the United States*, unclassified version, Washington, D.C., March 31, 2005.

Springall, Drew, Travis Finkenauer, Zakir Durumeric, Jason Kitcat, Harri Hursti, Margaret MacAlpine, and J. Alex Halderman, "Security Analysis of the Estonian Internet Voting System," *CCS '14: Proceedings of the 2014 ACM SIGSAC Conference on Computer and Communications Security*, November 2014, pp. 703–715.

Thomson, James C., "How Could Vietnam Happen? An Autopsy," *The Atlantic*, April 1968.

Ukrainian Election Task Force, *Foreign Interference in Ukraine's Democracy*, Washington, D.C.: Atlantic Council, May 2019.

UK Security Service, "MI5's Law and Governance," webpage, undated. As of July 26, 2021:
https://www.mi5.gov.uk/law-and-governance

U.S.-China Economic and Security Review Commission, "Comprehensive List of the Commission's Recommendations," in *2019 Report to Congress of the U.S.-China Economic and Security Review Commission*, Washington, D.C.: U.S. Government Publishing Office, November 2019, pp. 537–545.

Vest, Jason, and Robert Dreyfuss, "The Lie Factory," *Mother Jones*, January/February 2004.

Vilmer, Jean-Baptiste Jeangène, and Heather A. Conley, *Successfully Countering Russian Electoral Interference: 15 Lessons Learned from the Macron Leaks*, CSIS Brief, Washington, D.C.: Center for Strategic and International Studies, June 2018.

Wang, Shirley S., Newley Purnell, and Suryatapa Bhattacharya, "Nepal Aid Workers Helped by Drones, Crowdsourcing," *Wall Street Journal*, May 1, 2015.

Weinbaum, Cortney, and John N. T. Shanahan, "Intelligence in a Data-Driven Age," *Joint Force Quarterly*, Vol. 90, 3rd Quarter, July 2018, pp. 4–9.

Williams, Heather J., and Ilana Blum, *Defining Second Generation Open Source Intelligence (OSINT) for the Defense Enterprise*, Santa Monica, Calif.: RAND Corporation, RR-1964-OSD, 2018. As of December 1, 2021:
https://www.rand.org/pubs/research_reports/RR1964.html

Woodruff Swan, Betsy, and Bryan Bender, "Spy Chiefs Look to Declassify Intel After Rare Plea from 4-Star Commanders," *Politico*, April 26, 2021.

Zegart, Amy, "The Moment of Reckoning: AI and the Future of US Intelligence," Hoover Institution, March 12, 2021a.

———, "Spies Like Us: The Promise and Peril of Crowdsourced Intelligence," *Foreign Affairs*, July/August 2021b.

Zulauf, Barry A., IC Analytic Ombudsman, Office of the Director of National Intelligence, "Independent IC Analytic Ombudsman's on Politicization of Intelligence," letter to the U.S. Senate Select Committee on Intelligence, Washington, D.C., January 6, 2021.